LEGAL RESEARCH
IN A NUTSHELL

By

MORRIS L. COHEN

Professor of Law and Law Librarian,
Harvard University Law School

SECOND EDITION

ST. PAUL, MINN.
WEST PUBLISHING CO.
1971

Cohen Legal Research 2nd Ed.
1—1971

PREFACE

The literature of American law is rich and varied and has a long and distinguished history. Its primary sources contain the rules of human behavior by which our society is governed; its ingenious finding tools provide access to the mass of chronologically published decisions and statutes; and its wide ranging secondary sources illuminate the law by study of its past, its present, and its future.

Legal literature, reflecting and shaping the continuing struggle for justice and order, is part of the cultural heritage of all men. But knowledge of its forms and skill in its use is even more certainly an essential part of the lawyer's basic training and equipment. This epitome of American legal bibliography is designed to assist the student in achieving such knowledge and skill. It is intended as an introduction where a fuller course of study, such as might be based on comprehensive texts like Price & Bitner's *Effective Legal Research*, Pollack's *Fundamentals of Le-*

gal Research, or Roalfe's *How to Find the Law,* is not offered. Since it is not intended to be a reference tool in any sense, footnotes and most bibliographic detail have been omitted. This *Nutshell* is rather designed to offer limited instruction through a simple, concise text and for best effect should be followed by some form of bibliographic exposure in a library setting. This can be done through the traditional legal research "finger exercises", through somewhat more analytical legal method problems, or through legal writing assignments.

This manual is based in large part on a previous edition for librarians which appeared as Volume 1, Number 2 of the DREXEL LIBRARY QUARTERLY under the title, *Legal Bibliography Briefed.* The author thanks Drexel University and its Graduate School of Library Science for permitting this publication. Appreciation is extended to former Dean Jefferson B. Fordham and to Dean Bernard Wolfman of the University of Pennsylvania School of Law whose administrations and colleagueship provided an atmosphere of encouragement for such work. The assistance and support received from my associates at the Biddle Law Library and my colleagues in other law libraries are also gratefully noted.

For their permission to reproduce exhibits from their respective publications, the author acknowledges the kindness of the Columbia University Legislative Drafting Research Fund, Commerce Clearing House, Inc., the Lawyers Co-operative Publishing Company, Shepard's Citations, the Edward Thompson Company, the Aspen Systems Corporation and the West Publishing Company.

And to the long-suffering law students who may be introduced to legal research through these pages, the book is dedicated.

July, 1971

MORRIS L. COHEN

*

TABLE OF CONTENTS

†

LEGAL RESEARCH IN A NUTSHELL

CHAPTER I

INTRODUCTION

In describing its forms and usages, we can divide legal literature into three categories: (a) primary sources; (b) search books or finding-tools; and (c) secondary materials.

Primary Sources. We can define the primary sources as those recorded rules of human behavior which will be enforced by the state. They include statutes passed by legislatures, decisions of courts, decrees and orders of executives, and regulations and rulings of administrative agencies.

American law today, as so construed, has a number of characteristics which should be noted for their bibliographic significance.

It is subject to constant change through new decisions (some 30,000 a year) and new statutes (at least 10,000 a year), requiring regular and prompt supplementation and updating.

Its development is marked, however, by a quest for certainty and stability, as reflected in the doctrine of *stare decisis,* which gives most law books a continuing relevancy long beyond their period of publication.

It derives from many governmental agencies (judicial, legislative and executive) and from a variety of jurisdictions (the federal government, 50 states and a host of local counties, cities and towns), multiplying the bibliographic *sources* of law in this country.

Its components differ in their relative authority—some are binding, others only persuasive in various degrees, and some lacking in any formal legal force—leading to a need for careful evaluation by the user.

Its forms are issued *chronologically* in either official or unofficial publications, requiring some means of access by subject to enable the researcher to find the law applicable to a particular factual situation.

Federal and state statutes and appellate court decisions are the most important primary authorities. Traditionally they were the only primary sources of law, administrative materials being considered secondary forms since their authority *derived* from the legislature. Only in the last generation, by virtue of their great impact on the legal system, have administrative regulations, orders, and decisions, been treated as primary sources.

The primary sources relevant to any problem may range in time from the first enactments of our law-making bodies to the most recent decisions, statutes and rulings. A current decision may be based on a precedent many generations old; an executive order may stem from a statute of another century. Since primary sources retain legal effect until expressly overruled or repealed, access to even the earliest sources is a continuing necessity.

Finding-Tools. Because of the great number of decisions and statutes issued since the beginning of our legal history and because of their chronological method of publication, the researcher needs some means of subject access into this large body of law. The effective operation of the doctrine of precedent requires that prior decisions be easily available. In legal research as in other facets of his work the lawyer employs what should be a highly developed sense of relevancy—a keen appreciation of what is legally and factually relevant to a particular problem. Without a topical approach to legal sources, he could not find existing statutes or decided cases in point. A varied group of finding-tools, typically issued by specialized private publishers, provide such access. These include digests of decisions, citators, encyclopedias, phrasebooks, annotated statutory compilations, looseleaf services, and indexes. Such research books may lack legal authority themselves, but provide the means of locating the primary sources of authority.

Secondary Materials. Finally, there is the last major component of legal bibliography, the secondary sources. These include textbooks, treatises, commentaries, restatements, and periodicals which explain and describe the law for the practitioner, the scholar and the student. They vary widely in quality, form and authority, ranging from monumental treatises by great academic scholars to superficial tracts by hack writers. Encyclopedias are sometimes considered to be in this group, although some scholars prefer treating them primarily as case finders and casting them with the finding-tools and search books.

Although these works lack legal authority in a formal sense, some may have a persuasive influence in the law-making process by virtue of the recognized prestige of their authors or quality of their scholarship. Access to these materials is usually provided by their own internal subject indexes, although a variety of separate indexes have been developed for periodicals and some guides and bibliographies are available for texts and treatises.

LAW LIBRARIES

There are many types of law libraries, serving many kinds of readers who are engaged in legal research for different reasons and with different approaches. These collections range in size and purpose from the million volume libraries at the Harvard Law School and the Law Library of Congress to the law office library of a thousand volumes serving a few practicing lawyers. They are also found in court houses, government agencies, corporations, bar associations, and even within public libraries.

Regardless of differences in size, purpose and clientele, most law libraries have a great deal in common. The following are the usual components of the larger law libraries:

Administrative Decisions, Regulations, and Reports

Appellate Records and Briefs

Attorneys General Opinions

Bar Association Reports and Proceedings

Bibliographies and Research Guides

Biographies

Citators to Cases and Statutes

Commentaries, Histories, and Surveys of Law

Constitutions, their Conventions and Histories

Dictionaries

Digests of Case Law

Directors of Lawyers and Law Firms

Encyclopedias

Executive Documents

Fiction and Anecdotes Relating to Law

Foreign and Comparative Legal Sources

Form-books

International Law Materials

Judicial Reporters

Legislative History and Sources

Looseleaf Services

Periodicals and their Indexes

Practice and Procedure Manuals

Reference Books—Legal and General

Restatements of the Law

Sourcebooks of Historical Documents

Statutes—Session Laws and Codes

Texts, Treatises and Monographs

Treaties

Trials

Access to the contents of law libraries may be facilitated in several ways: law librarians, who are often trained bibliographic specialists, offer expert direction; the specialized indexes and finding-tools described herein provide access to the primary sources of law; and the card catalog, that most neglected and ingenious tool of information retrieval, aids in identifying and locating most of the library's collection.

AIDS TO RESEARCH

Because legal bibliography differs from other bibliography, and legal research from research in general, several special aids are recommended. For an understanding and mastery of the language of the law, a good law dictionary is a necessity for the beginning student. The most recent editions of *Ballentine, Black* or *Bouvier* are the most popular.

To cope with the complex shorthand of legal citations, guides to proper citation form and usage are available. *A Uniform System of Citation,* published by the Harvard Law Review Association, and Price's *Practical Manual of Standard Legal Citations* are recommended.

Detailed information on the sources of American law can be found in the bibliographic treatises of *Price & Bitner, Pollack,* and *Roalfe,* referred to previously, and in particular in the detailed appendices to the first edition (1953) of *Price & Bitner.*

Legal sources have been more fully described and cataloged then perhaps any other literature. The bibliographic approaches of legal research are the most highly developed and sophisticated in pre-computer documentation. The brave new world of information science, which is currently dawning, may carry us even further, but the practitioners of legal research have never fully exploited the tools at hand. The widespread failure to use the many aids and shortcuts now available leads to that sad by-product of bibliographic ignorance—needless waste of valuable time and effort.

CHAPTER II

JUDICIAL REPORTS

Law reports, containing the decisions of courts, form one of the two great sources of legal authority. Although statutes are seemingly more direct and imperative, many say that they are ineffective until construed or interpreted by judges and actually applied to particular situations. The development of the recording of judicial decisions undoubtedly has been related to the quest for certainty in the law. In seeking to achieve regularity in the impact of legal rules, men have come to realize the value of recording the decisions of particular legal controversies. Such records not only aid in preventing further disputes, but may also provide guidance to later tribunals when faced with similar cases.

Karl Llewellyn formulated the following reasons for the doctrine of precedent:

" * * * laziness as to the re-working of a problem once solved; the time and energy saved by routine, especially under the pressure of business; the values of routine as a curb on arbitrariness and as a prop of weakness, inexperience and instability; and the social value of predictability; the

> power of whatever exists to produce ex-
> pectations and the power of expectations
> to become normative * * * that curi-
> ous, almost universal sense of justice which
> urges that all men are properly to be
> treated alike in like circumstances."
> (**"Case Law"** in the *Encyclopedia of Social
> Sciences,* 1937)

From its beginnings, law reporting facilitated
the achievement of those purposes and the
search for predictability. Only by written
records could the future impact of the law be
appraised and the conduct of men influenced
thereby. Whether or not that was the original rationale of law reporting, it certainly
has been its most important by-product.

In addition to their value as legal precedent
and their importance in legal bibliography
and research, the law reports constitute a
literary form with other values as well. They
describe human problems and predicaments
—domestic crises, moral failings, economic
troubles. They reflect the larger social, political and economic trends and conditions of
particular periods and places. And they frequently have a unique literary quality which
adds to the tone and body of the prose of
their time. Sometimes brilliant and sometimes dull, legal writing has always been an
influential part of general literature.

The earliest evidence of law reporting in England follows close on the Norman conquest of 1066; scattered records of judicial decisions exist from that period. The *Plea Rolls* beginning with Richard I in 1189 contain fragmentary reports, which have been republished and cited in later works. Many of the oldest cases, however, remain only in the synthesis of early legal texts, such as those by Glanville (c. 1190) and Bracton (1250).

The next collection of judicial reports is to be found in the *Yearbooks* which cover the long period from 1285 to 1537. These reports were actually written in court, by either law students or lawyers. Some represent verbatim transcripts of the proceedings; others are brief summaries of the decision. In their entirety they constitute a great body of legal literature, which has been edited and republished in scholarly series by the Selden Society and similar groups.

Following the *Yearbooks* came the *nominative* reporters, that is, court reports named for the particular man who recorded or edited them. The earliest of these was probably James Dyer whose reports were published around 1550 and covered cases from 1537. Plowden's Reports, which were first published in 1571, are considered to be among the finest and most accurate, while the reports of Sir Edward Coke were perhaps the most influential of that period. The *nominatives* continued until modern English law reporting began in 1865 with the establishment of the *Law Reports,* a quasi-official series of annual reporters for each of the four major English courts. These are still being published today in monthly parts along with two other comprehensive weekly reporters, *All England Law Reports* (1936 to date) and the *Weekly Law Reports* (1953 to date).

In 1900, to collect the earlier cases, the *English Reports, Full Reprint* published 100,000 of the most important reports covering the period from 1378 to 1865 in 176 volumes. This set and a later *Revised Reports* have become the major sources of decisions for that early period. Alphabetical tables of cases provided the primary means of access to these useful collections, although more sophisticated case finders have since been developed, as indicated in the next chapter.

Among all of the foreign legal systems, that of England still has a special relevance in this country by virtue of our common legal history. The American colonies inherited the English Common Law and a legal tradition of statutes, cases, customs, and attitudes. With exclusions of what was repugnant to American experience, this inheritance was made express by the reception statutes enacted in many of the states upon their independence. Although we have increasingly gone our separate ways, English law and legal scholarship have continued to exert a persuasive influence here. The development of English law reporting has similarly shaped our own experience in that regard.

AMERICAN FEDERAL LAW REPORTING

Reports of The U. S. Supreme Court

The early development of American reports followed the pattern of the British reports of the same period. While nominative reporting was still the common practice in England, the first American reports were also issued by, and under the name of, individual reporters, beginning with Kirby's Reports in Connecticut in 1789.

Official court reporting began in 1790 with the inception of the *United States Reports,* which today is still the official edition of United States Supreme Court decisions. Alexander J. Dallas was the Court's first official reporter and issued the first four volumes of the *U. S. Reports,* covering the period from 1790 to 1800. Citations to the early volumes of the *U. S. Reports* must include the name of the particular reporter, but after volume 90 (1874), they are normally cited only by volume number of the *U. S. Reports.* Thus the official citation of *Mallory v. United States,* a 1957 decision on criminal confessions, is 354 U.S. 449 (1957), meaning the case beginning on page 449 of volume 354 of the *U. S. Reports.* The opening page of the official report of the *Mallory* case appears below in Exhibit 1.

A similar form of citation, including case name and date, is used for all court reports, whether state or federal, official or unofficial. In practice, most attorneys include in their citations parallel references to the unofficial reporters, although it is not necessary.

In addition to the official *U. S. Reports,* there are also two privately published editions of the Supreme Court's decisions which provide special research aids and supplementary material not in the official edition. These unofficial editions, described below, reproduce the same text of decisions as the official reports and often include more decisions than the official.

MALLORY *v.* UNITED STATES.

CERTIORARI TO THE UNITED STATES COURT OF APPEALS FOR
THE DISTRICT OF COLUMBIA CIRCUIT.

No. 521. Argued April 1, 1957.—Decided June 24, 1957.

Petitioner was convicted in a Federal District Court of rape and
sentenced to death after a trial in which there was admitted in
evidence a confession obtained under the following circumstances:
He was arrested early in the afternoon and was detained at police
headquarters within the vicinity of numerous committing magis-
trates. He was not told of his right to counsel or to a preliminary
examination before a magistrate, nor was he warned that he might
keep silent and that any statement made by him might be used
against him. Not until after petitioner had confessed, about 9:30
p. m., was an attempt made to take him before a committing
magistrate, and he was not actually taken before a magistrate until
the next morning. *Held:* This was a violation of Rule 5 (a) of
the Federal Rules of Criminal Procedure, which requires that an
arrested person be taken before a committing magistrate "without
unnecessary delay," and the conviction is reversed. *McNabb* v.
United States, 318 U. S. 332; *Upshaw* v. *United States,* 335 U. S.
410. Pp. 449–456.

98 U. S. App. D. C. 406, 236 F. 2d 701, reversed and remanded.

William B. Bryant argued the cause for petitioner.
With him on the brief were *Joseph C. Waddy* and
William C. Gardner.

Edward L. Barrett, Jr. argued the cause for the United
States. With him on the brief were *Solicitor General
Rankin, Assistant Attorney General Olney, Beatrice
Rosenberg* and *Julia P. Cooper.*

MR. JUSTICE FRANKFURTER delivered the opinion of the
Court.

Petitioner was convicted of rape in the United States
District Court for the District of Columbia, and, as

Exhibit 1: The official *U. S. Reports,* showing the
official syllabus.

354 U.S. 449
Andrew R. MALLORY, Petitioner,

v.

UNITED STATES of America.

No. 521.

Argued April 1, 1957.

Decided June 24, 1957.

Rape prosecution. The United States District Court for the District of Columbia entered judgment of conviction, and defendant appealed. The United States Court of Appeals for the District of Columbia Circuit, 98 U.S.App. D.C. 406, 236 F.2d 701, affirmed, and the defendant brought certiorari. The Supreme Court, Mr. Justice Frankfurter, held that where it appeared that defendant was not promptly arraigned as required by Federal Rule of Criminal Procedure, admission of defendant's confession was improper.

Reversed and remanded.

1. Courts ⬦383(1)

Where important question involving interpretation of Federal Rules of Criminal Procedure was involved in capital case, Supreme Court granted petition for certiorari. Fed.Rules Crim.Proc. rule 1 et seq., 18 U.S.C.A.

4. Criminal Law ⬦264

The requirement of Federal Rule of Criminal Procedure that arraignment be "without unnecessary delay" is part of procedure devised by Congress for safeguarding individual rights without hampering effective and intelligent law enforcement. Fed.Rules Crim.Proc. rule 5(a), 18 U.S.C.A.

5. Criminal Law ⬦264

The provision of Federal Rule of Criminal Procedure requiring that arraignment be "without unnecessary delay" contemplates a procedure that allows arresting officers little more leeway than the interval between arrest and the ordinary administrative steps required to bring a suspect before nearest available magistrate. Fed.Rules Crim. Proc. rule 5(a), 18 U.S.C.A.

6. Arrest ⬦63(4)

The police may not arrest on mere suspicion but only on probable cause.

7. Criminal Law ⬦264

The next step in proceeding after person has been arrested is to arraign the arrested person before a judicial officer as quickly as possible so that he may be advised of his rights and so that the issue of probable cause may be promptly determined. Fed.Rules Crim. Proc. rule 5(a), 18 U.S.C.A.

Exhibit 2: The unofficial *Supreme Court Reporter,* showing the West Publishing Company's unique key number system of headnotes.

Supreme Court Reporter incorporates West Publishing Company's key number digest system, which purports to index the significant points of law in all reported appellate decisions under 420 broad legal topics and thousands of detailed sub-topics. Thus decisions appearing in the *Supreme Court Re-*

porter and in all of West's other reporters are preceded by headnotes containing short abstracts of the legal issues in that case. Each headnote is classified by the name of the digest topic and sub-topic numbers (called *key* numbers) which are assigned to the points of law in that case. The opening page of the *Mallory* case as it appears in the *Supreme Court Reporter* at 77 S.Ct. 1356 is shown in Exhibit 2 above illustrating these headnotes.

Lawyers' Edition of the U. S. Supreme Court Reports is published by Lawyers Co-operative Publishing Company as a sister publication to *American Law Reports (A.L.R.)* and *American Law Reports—Federal,* annotated reporters of selected state and federal cases. *Lawyers' Edition,* as it is called, offers another contribution to the reporting of U. S. Supreme Court decisions by including legal analyses in the form of annotations to some of the more important decisions. In addition, only this reporter carries summaries of counsels' arguments. The texts of the Supreme Court's decisions are, of course, identical with those in the other two editions. Exhibits 3, 4, and 5 show the opening page of the *Mallory* case in *Lawyers' Edition,* the beginning of the annotation and the summary of counsel's arguments therein which deal with the legal issues of that case. The annotations in *Lawyers' Edition* are supplemented with later citations and comments in the *Lawyers' Edition (2d series) Later Case Service.*

---

*[354 US 449]
•ANDREW R. MALLORY, Petitioner,

v

UNITED STATES OF AMERICA

354 US 449, 1 L ed 2d 1479, 77 S Ct 1356

[No. 521]

Argued April 1, 1957.   Decided June 24, 1957.

SUMMARY

The defendant, a 19-year-old lad of limited intelligence, was arrested by the police on suspicion of rape. Even though the police had ample evidence from other sources than the defendant for regarding him as a chief suspect, they first questioned him for approximately a half hour, then asked him to submit to a lie detector test, and to another such test after four hours of further detention. He was not told of his right to counsel or to a preliminary examination before a magistrate, nor was he warned that he might keep silent and that any statement made by him might be used against him. Although arraignment could easily have been made, the police did not arraign him until he had confessed. At his trial in the United States District Court for the District of Columbia the confession was introduced in evidence and he was convicted, the jury imposing the death sentence. The United States Court of Appeals for the District of Columbia Circuit affirmed (98 App DC 406, 236 F2d 701).

On certiorari, the United States Supreme Court reversed. In an opinion by FRANKFURTER, J., the court unanimously held that the confession obtained under the circumstances above was inadmissible. Particular reliance was placed on the fact that it was obtained while the defendant was unlawfully detained in violation of Rule 5(a) of the Federal Rules of Criminal Procedure, requiring that a person under arrest be taken to a committing magistrate without unnecessary delay.

SUBJECT OF ANNOTATION
Beginning on page 1735, infra
Admissibility of pretrial confession in criminal case

HEADNOTES
Classified to U.S. Supreme Court Digest, Annotated

Criminal Law § 57 — arraignment — purpose of Rule.
1. The requirement of Rule 5(a) of the Federal Rules of Criminal Procedure that a person under arrest be taken to a committing magistrate without unnecessary delay is part of the procedure devised by Congress for safeguarding individual rights without hampering effective and intelligent law enforcement.

Criminal Law § 57 — federal practice — arraignment.
2. Under Rules 4 and 5 of the Federal Rules of Criminal Procedure arresting officers are allowed little more leeway than the interval between arrest and the ordinary administrative steps required to bring a suspect before the nearest available magistrate.

Exhibit 3:   The *Lawyers' Edition* report showing its syllabus and headnotes.

ANNOTATION

Admissibility of pretrial confession in criminal case—Supreme
Court cases

[See US Digest, Anno: Evidence §§ 680–685.]

I. Introduction, scope, and summary

§ 1. Introduction and scope.

This annotation supersedes the ones in 93 L ed 115, 96 L ed 56, and 97 L ed 1555.

The object of the present annotation is to discuss the decisions of the United States Supreme Court involving the question[1] whether a defendant's[2] pretrial confession of guilt,

---

1. The question has been given much attention in recent legal literature. See, for instance, notes in 21 U of Cinn L Rev 192, 198 (1952); 14 Ga Bar J 486 (1952); 50 Mich L Rev 567, 772 (1952); 25 Southern Cal L Rev 215 (1952); 29 Ind LJ 151 (1954).

See also the articles cited in § 18, infra, footnote 2.

2. For a case holding that the extra-judicial confession of a third person, since deceased, that he had committed the murder with which the accused was charged, was not admissible in evi-

---

Exhibit 4: Part of the opening page of the annotation in *Lawyers' Edition* on the *Mallory* case.

ANDREW R. MALLORY, Petitioner,

v

UNITED STATES OF AMERICA

The case is reported in 1 L ed 2d 1479.

Annotation, p. 1735, supra.

BRIEFS AND APPEARANCES OF COUNSEL

William B. Bryant, of Washington, D. C., argued the cause, and, with Joseph C. Waddy and William C. Gardner, also of Washington, D. C., filed a brief for petitioner:

An alleged confession obtained from a defendant who is a 19-year-old near-moron, at the end of a period of 7 or 8 hours of detention without the benefit of counsel, during which time he is subjected to repeated questioning in the face of repeated denials of complicity, and is finally subjected to a lie detector test and more questioning by federal officers for the very purpose of securing an incriminating statement, during which time the accused could have been taken before a readily accessible committing authority, is inadmissible in a criminal proceeding in a federal court. See McNabb v United States, 318 US 332, 87 L ed 819, 63 S Ct 608; Upshaw v United States, 335 US 410, 93 L ed 100, 69 S Ct 170; Brown v Allen, 344 US 443, 97 L ed 469, 73 S Ct 397; Stein v New York, 346 US 187, 97 L ed 1544, 73 S Ct 1077. See also Akowskey v United States, 81 App DC 353, 158 F2d 649.

"Unnecessary delay" does not depend upon the time desired to keep a suspect away from the committing magistrate for the purpose of interrogation and investigation and making a case against him, but rather upon the time required to bring the suspect before committing magistrate. See United States v Leviton (CA2d NY) 193 F2d 848 (dissent op). The lower court's interpretation seems to be squarely in conflict with the decisions of this Court and the general legislative policy underlying Rule 5.

Under the McNabb (318 US 332, 87 L ed 819, 63 S Ct 608) and Upshaw (335 US 410, 93 L ed 100, 69 S Ct 170) decisions, a confession obtained at the end of a period of detention during which the petitioner is withheld from presentment solely for the purpose of obtaining such confession is illegal.

Exhibit 5: Part of the page showing Briefs of Counsel in *Lawyers' Edition*.

The complete citation of the *Mallory* decision, reflecting all three texts, is *Mallory v. United States,* 354 U.S. 449, 77 S.Ct. 1356, 1 L.Ed.2d 1479 (1957). This form is widely used, although technically the official citation is sufficient. The "2d" in the citation of *Lawyers' Edition* indicates that those reports are now in a second series, an arbitrary numbering technique employed by most publishers of court reports. When the volumes of a reporter reach a certain number (usually volume 300, but in the case of *Lawyers' Edition,* volume 100), the publisher starts a second series and begins numbering from volume 1 again. If a report is in its second series, that must be indicated in its citation in order to distinguish it from the same volume number in the first series.

The bound volumes of these three reporters of Supreme Court decisions are really, however, the last form of publication. The following services, presented here chronologically, provide the text of such decisions much sooner:

Loose-leaf Services. Two unofficial commercial publications, issued in loose-leaf form, publish the Supreme Court's decisions on the day after they are announced, so that many of their subscribers have them within 48 hours. These loose-leaf services are *U. S. Law Week*, published by the Bureau of National Affairs, and *Supreme Court Bulletin,* published by Commerce Clearing House. Both of these publishers issue loose-leaf services on other legal topics as well, which will be discussed in detail in Chapter VII below. In addition to the prompt publication and delivery of the text of the decisions themselves, *U. S. Law Week* and *Supreme Court Bulletin* provide information about court calendars, dockets, motions, arguments, and general court news. They are extremely valuable to practitioners before the Supreme Court and of interest to legal researchers generally as a source of current information about the business of the Court. *U. S. Law Week* also includes another volume called *General Law*, which summarizes important weekly legal developments of all kinds—state and federal; judicial, legislative and administrative.

Slip Decision. Shortly after the unofficial loose-leaf services appear, the official slip decision of the Supreme Court is issued by the Court itself and usually reaches subscribers a week or two after decision date. This is the first official and authoritative text of the decisions, but its pages are not numbered in final form. Each slip decision is a separate pamphlet, paginated separately. They are available individually or by subscription from the U. S. Government Printing Office. These decisions are accumulated until there are enough for publication together as the advance sheet (or *preliminary print,* as it is officially called) of the official *U. S. Reports.*

Advance Sheets. Each of the reporters of the Supreme Court's decisions (and many other court reports) issues a preliminary booklet, which contains the Court's latest decisions in a temporary form during the term. These pamphlets are called "advance sheets" and are issued periodically so that attorneys may have the text of decisions without having to wait for the accumulation and publication of a complete bound volume. The pagination of the advance sheets is the same as that in the bound volume, so that cases can be cited from the advance sheet exactly as they will appear when finally published.

The advance sheets of *Supreme Court Reporter* and *Lawyers' Edition* are usually issued faster than the official *preliminary print* and all three include to some extent the unique features of the series to which they belong. The *preliminary print* is the authoritative text of the Court's decisions until the bound volume of the *U. S. Reports* appears; *Supreme Court Reporter* incorporates West's unique key number digest; the *Lawyers' Edition* advance sheet provides subscribers with a prompt text of Supreme Court decisions, but does not contain the annotations or the summaries of briefs and arguments found in the bound volume, since they cannot be prepared that rapidly.

Bound Volumes. Finally, at the end of each term, the bound volumes of the three series are published. The identical text of the Court's decisions is contained in each and the two unofficial reporters also contain citations to the volume and page of the official report so that an attorney using them will be able to cite to the official report, as required by the Court. Occasionally the unofficial reporters manage to pick up a few minor motion decisions or memorandum rulings, which may not have been reported officially, thereby permitting them to claim somewhat greater coverage than the official series.

Lower Federal Court Reporting

During most of the 19th century, decisions of the U. S. District Courts and the U. S. Circuit Courts of Appeals were issued in over 200 separate series of *nominative* reports. Virtually every federal court published its own series and bibliographic chaos resulted from the impossibility of locating the reports of many courts anywhere but in its own locale or in the largest law libraries. Finally, in 1880, the West Publishing Company published a 30 volume series which included many of these decisions under the title *Federal Cases*. This closed set incorporated the most important lower federal court decisions from 1789 to 1880. At the same time, West initiated its *Federal Reporter* which began publishing decisions of both the district and circuit courts in 1880 and has continued to date. In 1931 with the increasing volume of litigation in the federal courts, West began another series of federal reports called *Federal Supplement* which since that time has published selected U. S. District Court decisions, leaving the *Federal Reporter* to cover the decisions of the various U. S. Circuit Courts of Appeals (now called U. S. Courts of Appeals). Each reporter now also includes a number of specialized federal courts. In 1940 West began still another series, *Federal Rules Decisions,* which offers a limited number of decisions of the federal courts relating to procedural matters, as well as speeches and articles dealing with procedural law in the federal courts.

The decisions of the U. S. District Courts and the U. S. Courts of Appeals (except for those of the U. S. Court of Appeals for the District of Columbia) do not appear in an official edition, other than as slip decisions issued by some of the courts themselves. There are neither official advance sheets, nor official bound volumes for these courts. Lawyers rely exclusively on *Federal Reporter, Federal Supplement* and *Federal Rules Decisions* and on the *American Law Reports– Federal,* a series begun by Lawyers Cooperative in 1969 to offer a selection of federal court decisions with annotations.

[25]

STATE REPORTS

American state reports are published in two forms: official reports, which are issued by the courts themselves as their authoritative text, and the unofficial reports. There are two general unofficial reporting systems —the West Publishing Company's comprehensive *National Reporter System* and Lawers Co-operative Publishing Company's selective *American Law Reports*.

The official reports are important to the researcher because they are authoritative and must be cited in legal briefs and memoranda. Citation to the unofficial report is optional and, if given, should follow the official reference. The unofficial reports, however, are very widely used and usually cited, because of their superior research aids, fuller coverage and faster publication. In fact, they have become much more popular than the less imaginatively produced official editions. Since the unofficial reports usually include references to the citation of the official report, the researcher can cite directly to the official text. This is frequently done by a method called "star paging" which indicates the official pagination in the text of the unofficial report.

1. National Reporter System. West's *National Reporter System* consists of a series of regional reporters which collectively publish most of the decisions issued by the appellate courts of the 50 states every year. It is certainly the most comprehensive approach to law reporting ever devised and sometimes includes more decisions than the official reports. Although the system suffers to some extent from its huge scope and bulk, the ingenious key number case-finding device has kept it fairly manageable.

The *National Reporter System* divides the country into seven regions: Atlantic, Pacific, North Eastern, South Eastern, North Western, South Western and Southern. The decisions of the appellate courts of the states in each of these regions are published together in one series of volumes. These series have been supplemented by West with separate reporters for the two most litigious states, *New York Supplement* and the *California Reporter,* which also include selected lower court decisions. These nine reporters, together with West's federal court reporters described above, comprise a uniform system which is tied together by the key number indexing and digesting scheme.

The original rationale of the *National Reporter System* was that contiguous states shared similar legal development and therefore lawyers in one state would be interested in the law of adjacent states. Despite this theory, the venture has flourished, largely because of the speed of publishing decisions of several states in groups, rather than individually; the greater number of decisions as compared with the official reports; and the case-finding advantages of the key number system. In addition, advance sheets for each of these reporters bring the decisions to the lawyer much faster than do the official reporters, which rarely offer such service. After four or five advance sheets appear, they are reissued on a better paper in a bound volume with the same pagination. The superseded advance sheet can then be discarded.

By examining a typical West advance sheet one can observe the features which make these reporters so useful in legal research:

Final pagination and official citation, if available.

Judicial highlights from recent state and federal decisions.

Parallel reference tables to official citations of recent decisions

Table of cases reported.

Table of statutes construed.

Table of rules construed.

Table of words and phrases.

Key number digest for cases in that issue.

Text of the decisions in full, including dissents.

Similarly, by analyzing a single decision in one of the advance sheets, one can get a general idea of the make-up of an appellate decision, as well as of the special reporting aids which West provides for its subscribers. Such analysis would reveal the following items:

Title or case name.

Other identifying data: docket number, date of decision, name of court and jurisdiction.

Syllabus or brief descriptive paragraph of the case: its holding, how it arose, facts, etc.

Brief statement of decision and notation of dissent, if any.

Headnotes summarizing the points of law discussed in the case with the identifying key numbers of the digest system.

Names of counsel and judges.

Full text of opinion, decision, and dissents, if any.

[29]

2. Official State Reports. Once one is familiar with case reporting in the *National Reporter System,* there is little that can be learned from the official reports. However, it should be remembered that the official report is the authoritative text and must be cited in briefs or memoranda. It is customary to give the official report before the unofficial in citing the case, for example, *Alberts v. California,* 138 Cal.App.2d Supp. 909, 292 P. 2d 90 (1955). The citation to the official *California Appellate Reports* precedes the unofficial *Pacific Reporter.* Note that both the official and unofficial reporters are in their second series.

Because of the success of the West system and for reasons of economy, a number of states have abandoned their official reporters and some of these have adopted the West reporter as official. West, in turn, has issued a separate edition of the decisions of some states by reproducing the pages of those decisions as they appeared in the West regional reporter and cumulating them into bound volumes with their original page numbering. The following states have given up their official reports and the list will undoubtedly continue to grow: Alaska, Delaware (after volume 59, 1971) Florida, Kentucky, Maine, Mississippi, Missouri, North Dakota, Oklahoma, Texas and Wyoming. The Appellate Reports for Illinois and Louisiana have also been discontinued in their official edition.

Most official reporters include only the reports of the high court for that state, usually called the supreme court. A few states (e. g., New York, California, Illinois and Pennsylvania) issue more than one series of official reports, because they have an intermediate appellate court and a heavy volume of litigation. It is interesting to note that in New York where there are three official series of reports (*New York Reports,* covering the Court of Appeals; *Appellate Division Reports* covering the Appellate Divisions of the Supreme Court; and *Miscellaneous Reports* covering a selection of the decisions of the various lower courts) one single West series, *New York Supplement,* publishes as many cases as the three official reporters. In addition, West's *North Eastern Reporter* also publishes the decisions of the N.Y. Court of Appeals, that state's highest court.

Neither official slip decisions nor advance sheets are very common on the state level.

3. Annotated Reports. While West purports to publish virtually all of the appellate decisions in the United States, Lawyers Co-

operative Publishing Company approaches
case reporting from a different point of view.
Their series, *American Law Reports,* is based
on the annotated reporting of a small selection of significant cases.   *A.L.R.*, as it is
called, includes only 500 carefully chosen
state court decisions, each of which is annotated with an editorial discussion of the law
of that case.   The annotation includes past
developments, the current law in all states on
that problem, and probable future trends.
The annotations are not prepared by independent scholars, but by reasonably competent editorial writers employed by the publisher.   *A.L.R.* is favored by many legal researchers for the exhaustive coverage in
many of its annotations.   Even though the
leading decision may be from another state,
its annotation provides a well-indexed survey of the law in all states.   By focusing on
those decisions which significantly affect legal development or facilitate the detailed editorial development of an important area of
law, the *A.L.R.* annotation frequently offers
quicker access to the leading cases than other
tools.

Before *A.L.R.* was developed in its present
form, various predecessors were published
with annotations of varying frequency and

quality. These include the following: (1) Trinity series (*American Reports, American Decisions,* and *American State Reports*), 1789–1911; (2) *American and English Annotated Cases,* 1906–1911; (3) *American Annotated Cases,* 1912–1918; (4) *Lawyers Reports Annotated,* 1888–1918; (5) *American Law Reports,* 1st series: 1918–1947; 2nd series: 1947 to 1965. *A.L.R.* is currently in its third series.

Subject access to the decisions and annotations of *A.L.R.* is provided by word indexes and digests similar to the West's Key Number Digest, but considerably more limited. In addition, supplemental services and, in the 3rd series, pocket parts provide access to later decisions and annotations and permit the researcher to up-date any relevant decisions or annotations with later citations. It should be noted that advance sheets are not issued for *A.L.R.,* since the annotations require time for preparation and there would be little value in issuing a temporary edition of the decisions alone.

4. Special Subject Reporters. There is another significant type of unofficial court reporting, which brings together cases in a particular subject area. Examples of such series are the *American Maritime Cases, Public Utilities Reports Annotated,* and *U. S. Patents Quarterly.* Some of these, like C.C.H. *Labor Cases* and Prentice-Hall's *American Federal Tax Reports,* are published as adjuncts to loose-leaf services on those topics. A few of these reporters also include decisions of administrative agencies in the same field.

LOCATING PARALLEL CITATIONS OF CASE REPORTS

Since there are several reporting systems publishing simultaneously, the same decision often appears both in the official reports and in the *National Reporter System*—occasionally it may also be in the *American Law Reports.* Frequently the researcher will have a citation to only one of these reports and will want to obtain citations to the others, either to complete his citation in a brief or to examine the other report.

For that purpose parallel citation tables, such as the following, are used:

1. Case Name. If the case name is known, the Table of Cases volume of the West Digest for the appropriate jurisdiction or period will include both the official and unofficial citation. Note the *Escobedo* case citations appearing in the following exhibit from the West *U. S. Supreme Court Digest:*

```
Ernest v. Riverview State Bank, Kan,
  73 SCt 212, 344 US 892, 97 LEd 690,
  den'g cert Riverview State Bank v.
  Ernest 198 F2d 876.
Erwin v. U S, CtCl, 97 US 392, 24 L
  Ed 1065—U S 111(7).
Escobedo v. State of Ill, Ill, 84 SCt
  1758, 378 US 478, 12 LEd2d 977—
  Const Law 266, 268;  Courts 397½;
  Crim Law 393(1), 409. 412.2(2)  538
  (3), 641.3, 641.4(2), 641.7(1);  Mun
  Corp 188.
Esenwein v. Commonwealth ex rel
  Esenwein, Pa, 64 SCt 639, 321 US
  782, 88 LEd 1075, den'g cert Com-
  monwealth ex rel Esenwein v. Esen-
  wein, 348 Pa 455, 35 A2d 335, va-
  cated 64 SCt 1282, 322 US 725, 88
  LEd 1562.
```

Exhibit 6: Table of Cases in the
           *U. S. Supreme Court
           Digest.*

2. Popular Name. If the case has acquired through common usage a popular name, it can be traced through that designation in popular name tables published by Shepard's Citations. Originally published by Shepard's in pamphlet form, a separate Shepard's volume was issued in 1968 entitled *Shepard's Acts and Cases by Popular Names —Federal and State.* That volume is being updated by pamphlet supplements. The following exhibit illustrates entries in the case section of that volume:

Den	FEDERAL AND STATE CASES CITED BY POPULAR NAMES

Denver Water Company Cases
246 US 178, 62 LE 649, 38 SC 278
187 Fed 800, 110 CCA 24; 225 US
707, 56 LE 1266, 32 SC 839; 229
US 123, 57 LE 1101, 33 SC 657

Desegregation Cases
32 DelCh 343, 87 A2d 862; 33 DelCh
144, 91 A2d 137; 344 US 891, 97
LE 689, 73 SC 213; 345 US 972, 97
LE 1388, 73 SC 1118; 347 US 483,
98 LE 873, 74 SC 686; 348 US 886,
75 SC 210; 349 US 294, 99 LE 1083,
75 SC 753; 349 US 914, 75 SC 602
98 FS 529; 342 US 350, 96 LE 392, 72
SC 327; 103 FS 920; 344 US 1, 97
LE 3, 73 SC 1; 345 US 972, 97 LE
1388, 73 SC 1118; 347 US 483, 98
LE 873, 74 SC 686; 348 US 886,
75 SC 210; 349 US 294, 99 LE
1083, 75 SC 753; 349 US 914, 75
SC 602
98 FS 797; 344 US 1, 97 LE 3, 73 SC
1; 344 US 141, 97 LE 152, 73 SC
124; 345 US 972, 97 LE 1388, 73
SC 1118; 347 US 483, 98 LE 873,
74 SC 686; 348 US 886, 75 SC 210;
349 US 294, 99 LE 1083, 75 SC 753
103 FS 337; 344 US 1, 97 LE 3, 73 SC
1118; 347 US 483, 98 LE 873, 74
SC 686; 348 US 886, 75 SC 210;
349 US 294, 99 LE 1083, 75 SC 753

Dirty Stock Case
227 F2d 737; 127 FS 790; 351 US 919,
100 LE 1451, 76 SC 712

Discounted Salt Case
162 F2d 949; 332 US 850, 92 LE 420,
68 SC 355; 334 US 37, 92 LE 1196,
68 SC 822

Discrimination Law Case
116 NYSupp2d 264; 282 AppDiv 353,
122 NYSupp2d 721; 307 NY 38, 119
NE2d 581

Discriminatory Landlord Case
190 Misc 187, 74 NYSupp2d 220; 274
AppDiv 992, 85 NYSupp2d 313;
290 NY 512, 87 NE2d 541; 339 US
981, 94 LE 1385, 70 SC 1019; 70
SC 243

Dispensary Cases
41 SCar 220, 19 SE 458

Distilled Spirits Case
78 US 356, 20 LE 167

District Court Case
34 OhioSt 431

Ditty Case
286 Ky 395, 150 SW2d 672

Exhibit 7:   *The case table in Shepard's Acts and Cases by Popular Names.*

Popular names of cases are also listed separately in the main table of cases of many digests.

3. From Official to Unofficial Report, that is, where the official citation is known and the unofficial is sought, one can use either of the following:

(a) *National Reporter Blue Book* (or the State Blue & White Books) which are issued by West for this purpose:

406 PENNSYLVANIA REPORTS

Pa.	A.2d		Pa.	A.2d		Pa.	A.2d		Pa.	A.2d	
Pg.	Vol.	Pg.	Pg.	Vol.	Pg.	Pg.	Vol.	Pg.	Pg.	Vol.	Pg.
133	176	445	207	177	496	363	178	574	452	178	705
134	176	630	229	177	809	370	178	560	455	179	197
137	176	413	259	176	906	376	178	605	465	178	578
140	176	450	268	177	619	384	178	615	476	178	549
142	176	644	272	177	493	387	177	450	484	178	502
145	177	451	277	177	491	389	178	547	493	178	758
147	176	430	281	177	621	393	178	595	501	178	591
149	176	426	283	177	616	395	178	691	508	178	567
152	177	82	290	177	824	396	178	613	515	178	751
158	176	645	315	178	145	400	178	696	522	178	736
163	176	632	322	178	768	402	178	742	528	178	722
168	176	653	337	178	716	413	179	649	534	179	240
184	177	453	339	178	740	422	178	699	538	179	231
188	176	400	343	178	728	427	178	609	539	178	617
197	176	664	359	178	693	431	178	762	543	178	611
206	177	97	361	177	447	438	179	209	547	177	448

Exhibit 8: *Part of an entry in the National Reporter Blue Book.*

(b) Shepard's state citations—the first citation in the listing of each case refers to the alternate report of the case in the regional reporter. That parallel citation is usually in parentheses.

```
                    MASSACHUSETTS REPORTS
                —71—    335Mas4677   19A3 471s   —210—
 Vol. 335    (138NE581)  342Mas 770  96A3  915n  (139NE393)
             335Mas1707    —128—       —170—     336Mas2694
   —1—          —78—    (138NE354)  (138NE635)  348Mas2459
(138NE276)   (138NE609)  342Mas1391  72A3  123n    —216—
345Mas1402   338Mas 550  342Mas 768    —172—     (139NE385)
   —6—       339Mas3662    —130—     (138NE751)  348Mas1467
(138NE200)   339Mas 668  (138NE586)  338Mas  19    —220—
338Mas1572   342Mas4418  s340Mas 132 339Mas1778  (139NE407)
   —9—       345Mas4532  335Mas2543  339Mas1780  21A3   95s
(138NE280)   346Mas6568  335Mas3745  344Mas124   67A3   21n
335Mas 425  j347Mas1227  336Mas3463  344Mas1385  67A3   97n
336Mas 197   348Mas2656  336Mas2764  345Mas1534    —223—
336Mas2267   44MQ(2) 17  337Mas2603  346Mas1274  (139NE715)
345Mas1770   39A3  209s  337Mas2613   9A3  938s  340Mas1729
348Mas1436   43A3 1072s  d338Mas3178  16A3   3s  19A31228s
68YLJ639        —84—     339Mas 200    —175—       —228—
   —12—      (138NE373)  340Mas3282  (138NE762)  (139NE387)
(138NE278)   339Mas1483  340Mas3781  337Mas 508  335Mas1738
165FS 7737   345Mas1716  341Mas3263  338Mas5162  372US1732
   —19—      167FS 1922  343Mas 724
```

Exhibit 9: From *Shepard's Massachusetts Citations.*

4. From Unofficial to Official Report:

(a) State Blue and White books, issued by West for 33 states to provide parallel citations from the official reports to the *National Reporter System*. White pages also carry citation tables from the unofficial to the official report. These books are available to law libraries only for the state in which they are located. Their arrangement is similar to that in the *National Reporter Blue Book*. (Exhibit 8).

(b) Shepard's regional reporter citations —the first entry, in parentheses, is to the *official* report.

```
NORTHEASTERN REPORTER, 2d SERIES (Massachuset
—924—        |           | 172NE 6271 | —376—       | —605—
Case 1       | Vol. 138  | 197NE 4700 | (335Mas760) | (335Mas 80)
(334Mas708)  |           | —270—      | —567—       | —606—
—924—        | —115—     | Case 1     | (334Mas637) | (335Mas701)
Case 2       | (334Mas697)| (334Mas709)| —570—      | —607—
(334Mas708)  | 172NE 3821 | —270—     | (335Mas 41 | (335Mas38)
cc137NE 923  | —118—     | Case 2     | 171NE844   | 175NE 2484
—925—        | (334Mas677)| (334Mas693)| —576—     | —609—
Case 1       | —120—     | —273—      | (335Mas162)| (335Mas 78)
(334Mas708)  | (334Mas652)| (334Mas684)| 178NE 2870| 153NE 7624
—925—        | 148NE 6390 | 146NE 3511 | 106NE 4027| 162NE 7268
Case 2       | 153NE 4771 | 173NE 3643 | 338F2d1646| 162NE 274
(334Mas610)  | 173NE 5292 | 202NE 3598 | —578—     | 173NE 5815
151NE 484    | —124—     | —276—      | (335Mas101)| 188NE 6576
181NE 4659   | (334Mas624)| (335Mas 1)| 138NE 4775| 194NE 8705
d196FS 4617  | 146NE 2509 | 187NE1845 | 141NE 2839| j107NE 3587
             | 149NE 2904 | —280—     | 142NE2328 | 205NE3231
             | 170NE 1358 | (335Mas 9)| 149NE 2907| —613—
             |           | 140NE 660  |           |
```

Exhibit 10: From *Shepard's Northeastern Reporter Citations*.

(c) The official citation is also supplied at the beginning of the case in the regional reporter, if it is available at the time of printing.

CHAPTER III

CASE–FINDING

The doctrine of precedent is effective only if judicial decisions are published and kept easily available, so that they can be cited by lawyers and used by courts in deciding later cases. In order to discover what is the applicable law, lawyers must have some means of locating "cases in point," that is, earlier decisions which are factually and legally relevant to the cases on which they are working. They must be able to locate precedents with which they can support their positions and persuade a court to accept their arguments. However, as we have seen, judicial decisions are published in chronological order, both in their official and unofficial reports. This body of law, consisting of almost three million decisions to which are added approximately thirty thousand new decisions every year, could hardly be searched for relevant precedents, unless there were some means of subject access.

Such access is, in fact, provided by various finding-tools—the most important of which are case digests. A digest to judicial decisions superimposes a subject classification upon chronologically published cases. The classification consists of an alphabetically arranged scheme of legal topics and subtopics which can be approached through a detailed index. Brief abstracts of the points of law in decided cases are classified by subject and set out in the digests under appropriate topical headings. They are then located and retrieved by the researcher through the index to the digest.

As soon as comprehensive case reporting began to develop in England, finding-tools were published to provide a topical approach. Initially this function was performed by texts, but then abridgments and digests were devised to enable lawyers to find relevant prior cases on particular topics. These finding-tools were alphabetical arrangements of brief abstracts of important court decisions set out under broad legal topics. One of the earliest of these was *Statham's Abridgment* printed around 1490. Later important abridgments were made by Fitzherbert (1514); Brooke (1568); Rolle (1668); Jacobs (1713); Bacon (1736); and Viner (1742). The early abridgments and digests were prototypes of the modern digests, but used only a few broad topics and included a relatively small number of decisions. Gradually these finding-tools grew more and more intensive, employing finer internal subdivisions, and more and more extensive, covering more areas of law and a larger number of cases.

WEST DIGESTS

Today the digests of the West Publishing Company constitute the most comprehensive subject approach to case law. For this purpose, West has divided American law into some 420 broad topics, which are then subdivided into hundreds and thousands of detailed sub-topics. Each such sub-topic bears the name of the broad topic and a key number designating its specific subdivision. This topical breakdown is illustrated by the analysis of the topic "Bigamy," a rather short topic, appearing in Exhibit 11 below:

BIGAMY

Scope-Note.

INCLUDES marriage of a person, who has a husband or wife living, to another person; nature and extent of criminal responsibility therefor, and grounds of defense; and prosecution and punishment of such marriages as public offenses.

Matters not in this topic, treated elsewhere, see Descriptive-Word Index.

Analysis.

- 1. Nature and elements of offense.
- 2. Defenses.
- 3. Indictment or information.
- 4. —— Requisites and sufficiency.
- 5. —— Issues, proof, and variance.
- 6. Evidence.
- 7. —— Presumptions and burden of proof.
- 8. —— Admissibility in general.
- 9. —— Previous marriage.
- 10. —— Illegal marriage or cohabitation.
- 11. —— Weight and sufficiency.
- 12. Trial.
- 13. —— Questions for jury.
- 14. —— Instructions.
- 15. New trial.
- 16. Appeal and error.
- 17. Sentence and punishment.

---

1. Nature and elements of offense.

Library references

C.J.S. Bigamy § 1 et seq.

App.D.C. 1943. There must be some honest and effective effort made to ascertain truth before it can be claimed that conclusion of defendant, charged with bigamy, that first wife had obtained divorce had been reached in good faith. D.C.Code 1940, § 22–601.

Alexander v. U. S., 136 F.2d 783, 78 U.S. App.D.C. 34.

D.C.N.J. 1956. Where neither petitioner nor his wife was domiciled in Mexico at any time, Mexican divorce was invalid under New Jersey law, and, therefore, relationship, under New Jersey law, between petitioner and woman he subsequently married was bigamous and adulterous.

Petition of Da Silva, 140 F.Supp. 596.

sonally appearing at trial in Mexico, and thereafter petitioner entered into ceremonial marriage in New Jersey, his relationship with his second wife was not bigamous within intent of New Jersey criminal law. N.J.S.A. 2A:92–1.

Petition of Smith, 71 F.Supp. 968.

2. Defenses.

U.S.N.Y. 1948. Person domiciled in one state should not be allowed to suffer penalties of bigamy for living outside state with only one which state of his domicile recognizes as his lawful wife, and children born of only marriage which is lawful in state of his domicile should not carry stigma of bastardy when they move elsewhere. 28 U.S. C.A. § 1738; U.S.C.A.Const. art. 4, § 1.

Estin v. Estin, 68 S.Ct. 1213, 334 U.S. 541, 92 L.Ed. 1561, 1 A.L.R.2d 1412.

Exhibit 11: Scope-Note and Analysis of the topic *Bigamy* in West Digest.

Editorial workers at West abstract the significant points of law discussed in all cases published in the *National Reporter System* and the other West reporters, which together constitute virtually all of the appellate decisions handed down in the United States. Each of these abstracts, or "squibs" as they are called, is classified under one or another of the legal topics used for this purpose. Research under many topics may turn up cases dating from the 17th century down to those decided a few weeks ago. Although the coverage is primarily of appellate court decisions, selected lower court opinions from some jurisdictions are also included (e. g. those reported in *Federal Supplement* and *New York Supplement.*)

Each of the topics and sub-topics used in the digest system is assigned an individual topic name and key number, which in turn is used for the classification of the particular cases related to that topic. Some short topics like *Lotteries* or *Obscenity* employ relatively few subdivisions and key numbers, while other broader ones like *Constitutional Law* or *Criminal Law* may have thousands. West publishes digests of this kind for many jurisdictions, the most comprehensive of which is the American Digest System. It covers all decisions in all of West's reporters and is divided into separate units, each of which covers a ten year period, since the accumulation of all decisions for the entire country in one set would be unmanageable and require frequent revision.   These ten year units are called *Decennial Digests,* the last one of which, the Seventh Decennial, includes cases decided between 1956 and 1966. The first unit of the system, called the *Century Digest,* covers 1658 to 1896, when the volume of litigation was, of course, relatively small.   The following are the various units of the American Digest System:

Years	Digest Unit
1658–1896	Century Digest
1897–1906	First Decennial
1907–1916	Second Decennial
1916–1926	Third Decennial
1926–1936	Fourth Decennial
1936–1946	Fifth Decennial
1946–1956	Sixth Decennial
1956–1966	Seventh Decennial

In 1967, the General Digest, Fourth Series, began digesting cases and will continue doing so until 1976.   At that time a new Decennial will be compiled and a new General Digest series will be born, unless the present pattern is changed.

Each of the American Digest units includes cases appearing in all of West's reporters—the *National Reporter System,* the various federal reporters, and the few individual state reporters.   In addition, West also publishes smaller digests which cover in a single alphabet (or sometimes two) all of the decisions of smaller geographical units.   For example, there are such digests for each of the regional reporters series except South Western Reporter, for most of the states (e. g. *Abbott's New York Digest, Vale's Pennsylvania Digest,* etc.), for federal cases (the *Modern Federal Practice Digest*), and even one for the U. S. Supreme Court alone (*United States Supreme Court Digest*).   All of the cases which are digested in these publications appear in the all-inclusive American Digest System also.   For reasons of convenience and economy, West makes the smaller units available to practitioners, who may not need or want the full set.   The regional and state digests contain no more than can be found in the American Digest, however.   The same key numbers and topics are used in the local digests as are used in the main one and the researcher can move between them easily.

The basic unit of the West digest system is the "squib" or one sentence summary of each principle of law dealt with in each of the reported cases. Every summary is accompanied by the citation to the case in which it appears. The digest as a whole consists of a chain of these squibs, classified and arranged under their topic names and key numbers, as shown in Exhibit 12 below.

---

3 F Pr Dig—913   **ARREST** ☞70

For references to other topics, see Descriptive-Word Index

eral agent, such testimony, in absence of evidence of agent's intent to restrain and actual restraint of defendant, was insufficient to show an arrest pursuant to which search without warrant could properly be made. U.S.C.A.Const. Amends. 4, 5; 26 U.S.C.A. (I.R.C.1939) §§ 2591(a), 2593(a), 3234(a).

U. S. v. Waller, 108 F.Supp. 450.

D.C.Mich. 1950. A sheriff or other officer making an arrest for felony, has some discretion as to the means taken to apprehend offender, and to keep him safe and secure after such apprehension, and such discretion cannot be passed on by a court or jury in an action for injuries sustained by the one arrested unless such discretion has been abused through malice, wantonness, or a reckless indifference to the common dictates of humanity.

Moran v. Lumbermens Mut. Cas. Co., 92 F.Supp. 267.

The measure of force permissible in making an arrest for a felony and keeping felon in custody, is that which an ordinarily prudent and intelligent person with the knowledge and in the situation of the arresting officer would have deemed necessary.

to preserve peace at religious meeting held in city if he was satisfied that a breach of peace was reasonably apprehended, and when rioters gathered at place of such public meeting chief of police had statutory duty to go among rioters, or as near to them as possible, and command them in name of state to disperse, and if they did not immediately disperse he had duty to arrest them or cause them to be arrested, and for that purpose command aid of all persons present or within county. 22 Okl.St.Ann. § 102.

Downie v. Powers, 193 F.2d 760.

☞**70. Custody and disposition of prisoner.**

U.S.App.D.C. 1957. An arrested person may be "booked" by the police, but he is not to be taken to police headquarters in order to carry out a process of inquiry that lends itself, even if not so designed, to eliciting damaging statements to support the arrest and ultimately his guilt. Fed.Rules Crim.Proc. rule 5(a), 18 U.S.C.A.

Mallory v. U. S., 77 S.Ct. 1356, 354 U.S. 449, 1 L.Ed.2d 1479.

Exhibit 12: A page from *Modern Federal Practice Digest*, showing the *Mallory* case under key number Arrest 70.

[47]

Despite its unquestioned value as a case finder, the digest has the following shortcomings:

It contains no explanatory text or comment, but merely a series of separate unevaluated case digests.

It does not conveniently indicate change in the law, whether by statute or later decision.

It reflects much dicta and over-abstracts every case, so that the researcher must wade through a great deal of irrelevant material in order to get citations to significant authorities.

It does not contain the texts of primary authority, but only provides the means of finding such authority.

Occasionally the squibs do not accurately state the points of law they purport to contain. Thus, the attorney using a digest for case finding must locate and choose the relevant line of cases for study. He must then read the apparently relevant cases and synthesize those which appear *most* relevant to arrive at an understanding or statement of the applicable law. Finally, he updates his search and determines the current status and authority of the cases found, by using the appropriate volumes of *Shepard's Citations.*

The digesting process begins with the appearance of the squibs in numbered headnotes at the beginning of the reported decisions in each West reporter. These summaries are then printed by topic and key number in the Key Number Digest which appears in the front of the advance sheet of every West reporter and subsequently in their bound volumes. All of these squibs are then collected from the various reporters and published in monthly supplements to the General Digest. These monthly pamphlets are cumulated every four months into the bound volumes of the General Digest. As we have seen, every ten years the General Digest itself is cumulated into a new Decennial Digest.

The key numbers will be used for the same points of law and types of cases in each of the component parts of the digest system, from the most recent all the way back to the First Decennial covering 1897–1906. The original unit, the Century Digest (1658–1896), employs a slightly different numbering system, but a table in Volume 21 of the First Decennial bridges this discrepancy by providing references from the Century Digest key numbers to those in the First Decennial. In order to go back from the numbers of the First Decennial to those of the Century Digest, reverse cross references appear under each key number in the volumes of the First and Second Decennials.

The researcher who wants to use the digest must have some convenient way of locating the topic and key number relevant to his problem. Access to the digest is through one of the following approaches: (1) by the name of a particular case which is known to be in point (or through its headnotes); (2) by the relevant legal concept; or (3) by an analysis of the factual make-up of the problem.

1.   Via Tables of Cases or Case Headnotes. If the researcher already knows of a case in point, he can locate its citation and the key numbers assigned to it by using the Table of Cases volume or volumes for the appropriate unit of the West digest system. If he knows the jurisdiction in which the case was decided, he can go to the local digest for that state or region. Otherwise, he has to know in which decennial digest the case appears, since there is no overall table of cases for the entire American Digest System. From that decennial's table he can get a direct reference to the appropriate key numbers under which the points of law of that case have been indexed. With the relevant key numbers, it is easy to locate other earlier or later cases on the same topic in the body of the digest. If the Table of Cases does not contain those references, he can locate the report of the case by its citation in the Table of Cases, examine the headnotes in the reported decision, and obtain from them the appropriate key numbers for further search. If the researcher already has the complete citation of the case which he knows to be relevant, he can of course go directly to its report and obtain the relevant key numbers from its headnotes. By using the Table of Cases, however, one can also obtain parallel citations to the official report of the same case, the later history of the case (whether it was affirmed, reversed, or modified), and possibly a reference to an *A.L.R.* annotated report. Exhibit 6 at page 35 above illustrates a typical case name table in a West digest. It is difficult, however, to use the Table of Cases approach to the digest unless one knows the approximate date or jurisdiction of the case in question, since, as we have seen, there is no single table of cases covering the entire digest system.

2. Legal Concept. This method requires the researcher to select the legal topic used in the West digests which is most relevant to his problem. There is a list of these topics in front of each volume of the digest system and the searcher can run through the list, select the appropriate topic, turn to it in the digest and, by inspecting the detailed table of contents at the beginning of each particular topic (as in Exhibit 11 at page 43 above), find the appropriate key number. With that key number he can then proceed to locate other cases in point in the digest proper. This is a chancy method and obviously less desirable than the factual approach described below. It is also *inefficient* to search through the list of topics and then to examine the content analysis of the chosen topic in order to obtain the appropriate key number. A great deal of time and effort can be wasted through the use of this method, particularly where the relevant topic is a broad one like *Constitutional Law* or *Criminal Law.*

3. Factual or Descriptive Word Method. The most efficient procedure for case finding in the digest relies on the use of specific factual catch words derived from an analysis of the problem in question. These words are searched in the Descriptive Word Indexes of the West digests in order to find the appropriate key number and topic for that problem. Exhibit 13 below illustrates such an index in the *Modern Federal Practice Digest* covering the subject matter of the *Mallory* case.

It is usually much faster to use these alphabetical indexes, which contain many thousands of legally significant catchwords and phrases, rather than the less precise conceptual approach.

CONFECTIONS   1 F Pr D DWI—1006

Reference are to Digest Topics and Key Numbers

CONFECTIONS (Cont'd)
TRADE-MARKS and trade-names (Cont'd)
   Containers, frozen confection, infringement.
      Trade Reg 338, 356
   Descriptive color, package contents. **Trade Reg 349**
   Different products, same mark or, name.
      Trade Reg 365
   Evidence. **Trade Reg 577**
   Form, simulating coins. **Trade Reg 348**
   Navy, application to candy, descriptiveness.
      Trade Reg 15
   Use as unfair competition. **Trade Reg 501**
UNFAIR COMPETITION. **Trade Reg 437**
   Imitation of products. **Trade Reg 528**
   Substitution. **Trade Reg 426**
   Use of trade-marks and trade-names.
      Trade Reg 501
UNFAIR trade practices, candy manufacturer furnishing punchboards, jurisdiction. **Trade Reg 749**

CONFEDERACY
CONSPIRACY, see this index Conspiracy

CONFEDERATE BONDS
CONTRACT for sale of. **Contracts 136**
EQUAL protection of law. **Const Law 241**
INVESTMENT in by guardian. **Guard & W 53**

CONFEDERATION
RIGHTS and liabilities of United States as successor of. **U S 1**

CONFERENCE
CORPORATE reorganization, attorneys' fees and expenses. **Bankr 697(11), 698(2, 4)**
DRAFT boards, memorandum, inclusion in selectee's file. **Armed S 20.8(9)**
EMPLOYEE and employer, time spent as compensable as overtime under Fair Labor Standards Act. **Labor 1283**
EMPLOYER'S action against unions and conferences—
   Courts 405(12.9)
   Labor 763, 765
INDUSTRY conference, unfair trade practice rules. **Trade Reg 747**
PRE-TRIAL CONFERENCE, see this index Pre-Trial Conference
STEAMSHIP carriers, power of court to pass on validity of rate fixing agreement. **Ship 103**
UNITED STATES contracts, meals, cost plus fixed fee. **U S 70(18)**

CONFERENCE SYSTEM
CONSPIRACY to violate wire tapping provision of Communications Act, evidence. **Consp 47**

CONFESSION
ADMINISTRATIVE agency, judicial power to punish refusal to confess illegal act before agency. **Admin Law 901**
ADMISSIBILITY—
   Insurance, confession of one burning insured property. **Insurance 658**
ADMISSION in civil action. **Evid 207(4)**
ALLEGATIONS in notice of opposition to registration of trade-mark or trade-name. **Trade Reg 218**
COURTS-MARTIAL, see this index Courts-Martial
DEPORTATION proceedings, admissibility. **Aliens 54.1(3)**
DIVORCE suits, see this index Divorce
DRAFTS for military service, occupational deferment, false statement. **Armed S 40.1(16)**
FACTS confessed by exceptions to libel. **Adm 65**
INTERROGATORIES to parties, answers used as confession. **Fed Civ Proc 1536**
SEARCH not legalized by. **Searches 7(27)**
STATE statute on judicial confessions, effect in federal court. **Courts 363**

CONFESSION AND AVOIDANCE
GENERALLY—
   Fed Civ Proc 751-759
   ~~Pleading 78~~
~~Answer ... Reply. Plead 178~~
SPECIAL plea, pleading matter available under. **Plead 137**
STATEMENT of new matter constituting defense under code. **Plead 132**
STRIKING PLEADING. **Fed Civ Proc 1108-1116**
WAIVER of objection to imperfect pleading. **Plead 409(4)**

CONFESSION OF CRIME
ACCOMPLICES. **Crim Law 528**
ADMISSIBILITY in evidence in general. **Crim Law 516-538**
ADMISSION of confession in evidence as a reversible error. **Crim Law 1169(12)**
ARRAIGNMENTS prior to making of confessions. **Crim Law 264**
AUTHORITY, confessions made to persons in authority. **Crim Law 519(4)**
ASSAULT, evidence of assault by officers in unsuccessful attempt to extort confession. **Crim Law 338(7)**
BURDEN of proof of voluntary character. **Crim Law 531(1)**
CAUTION, duty to warn accused before receiving. **Crim Law 518**
CIVIL RIGHTS—
   Denied by extortion. **Civil R 1**
   Indictment for violating in extorting confession. **Civil R 15**
CODEFENDANTS. **Crim Law 528**

Exhibit 13: A page from the Descriptive Word Index in the *Modern Federal Practice Digest*.

There is a Descriptive Word Index for each decennial digest and for each state and regional digest. West recommends that in using this method the researcher obtain his search words by analyzing his problem into these components: (a) Parties; (b) Places and things; (c) Basis of action or issue; (d) Defenses; and (e) Relief sought. A sample case used by West involves a professional wrestling match in which the referee was thrown from the ring in such a way that he struck and injured plaintiff who was a front row spectator. West offers the following analysis of that problem to provide appropriate search words for the index:

(a) Parties—Spectator, Patron, Arena Owner, Wrestler, Referee, Promoter

(b) Places and Things—Wrestling Match, Amusement Place, Theater, Show

(c) Basis of Action or Issue—Negligence, Personal Injury to Spectator, Liability

(d) Defense—Assumption of Risk

(e) Relief Sought—Damages

With that analysis, the researcher can look up the most specific words and phrases in the Descriptive Word Index and thereby locate relevant key numbers and their cases covering that problem.

A.L.R. DIGEST

American Law Reports and its companion, *American Law Reports–Federal*, also provide subject access to their chronologically published reports and annotations by indexes and digests. The researcher can use the following methods, similar to those described above for the West system:

1. Case Name. Tables of cases are provided in the *A.L.R.* digests, from which one can obtain the complete citation, a topic and number for searching the *A.L.R.* digest, or direct reference to a relevant *A.L.R.* annotation.

2. Legal Concept. One can use the *A.L.R.* digests directly by selecting a relevant legal concept in the digest, searching its table of contents for a relevant subdivision, and then obtaining references to pertinent cases and annotations therein. This involves the same disadvantages as does that approach in the West digest system and is rarely used.

3. Word Index. The best means of access to *A.L.R.* is through the use of its special indexes, via the relevant words or phrases of the problem to be searched. *Word Indexes,* similar to the West *Descriptive Word Indexes*, are provided with the digests for *A.L.R.*

1st and 2d series.   A new *Quick Index*, published in 1965, partially supersedes the *Word Index* for *A.L.R.* 2d series and provides access directly to the relevant annotations in *A.L.R.* 2d series and, by an annually revised pocket supplement, to *A.L.R.* 3d series as well.   Since the old *Word Index* to the 2d series provided many more index entries and catchwords, it will still be a useful entree to the 2d series.

It should be noted that the *A.L.R.* digests and indexes are supplemented and kept up to date with the latest annotations and decisions.   The researcher updates his search in the *A.L.R.* supplemental services after he has located a helpful case or annotation, e. g. the *A.L.R.2d Later Case Service* provides later decisions supplementing all of the annotations in the 100 volumes of *A.L.R.*2d series and pocket parts to the individual volumes of *A.L.R.3d* update that series.

When one is searching for an *A.L.R.* annotation or updating one, it is best to use *A.L.R.* research tools.

ENCYCLOPEDIAS

Conditioned by the use of scholarly general encyclopedias, one tends to expect American legal encyclopedias to be equally scholarly reference works in the broad sense.   However, legal encyclopedias are generally less highly reputed, particularly in academic circles, and really function best as case-finders. Since the leading encyclopedias do not cover statutes to any significant extent, they tend to give a somewhat distorted view of the law in many areas. In addition they have a tendency to over-simplify and over-generalize which often does not accurately reflect the complexity of our changing law.

The two main encyclopedias of national scope are *Corpus Juris Secundum* (published by West) and *American Jurisprudence* (published by Lawyers Co-operative Publishing Co.), now in its second series. Since the voluminous footnotes to the articles in *Corpus Juris Secundum* and *American Jurisprudence 2d* contain thousands of case references, they can be used directly as finding-tools for that purpose. Each has separate index volumes, as well as topical indexes, to help the researcher locate relevant articles and the most applicable sections thereof. The encyclopedias do not, however, contain tables of cases, presumably because of the large number of cases cited. Not surprisingly, West's *C.J.S.* purports to carry in its footnotes virtually all of the decisions listed in the various West digests, while Lawyers Co-op's *Am.Jur.* provides similar access to the relevant annotations of *A.L.R.* and *A.L.R. –Federal.*

Illustrating an encyclopedia is the following page from *Corpus Juris Secundum* in Exhibit 14:

Exhibit 14: A Sample Page from *Corpus Juris Secundum.*

WORDS AND PHRASES

Another useful case-finding tool is *Words and Phrases*, an encyclopedia of definitions and interpretations of legally significant words and phrases, published in 46 volumes by West. This set consists of an alphabetical arrangement of thousands of words and phrases followed by abstracts of judicial decisions which have interpreted, defined or construed them. The abstracts are in the same form as the West digest squibs, containing a one sentence summary of the legal interpretation and the citation to the decision from which it is taken. A typical page looks like the sample in Exhibit 15 below.

Words and Phrases is supplemented by annual pocket parts inserted in the back of each volume and by Tables of Words Construed which appear in every West advance sheet and bound reporter for the cases therein.

OATH

Appeal to God
"Oath" is appeal by person to God to witness truth of what he declares, and in its broadest sense it includes any form of attestation by which party signifies that he is bound in conscience to act truthfully. In re Rice, 181 N.E.2d 742, 745, 748, 35 Ill.App. 2d 79.

Belief in God
Call on God to witness that what is said by witness is true and invoking divine vengeance on him, if what he says is false. Hudson v. State, 179 S.W.2d 165, 169, 207 Ark. 18.

Form or mode
Statute providing for transfer of cause from magistrate court to circuit court if defendant "by his 'oath' verifies the truth of the allegations of the counterclaim" wherein it is asserted there is amount in dispute beyond magistrate court jurisdiction may be satisfied by oral oath, and written verification is not required. State ex rel. May Dept. Stores Co. v. Weinstein, Mo.App., 395 S.W.2d 525, 527.

In administering "oath" to affidavit the law requires that there must be something done in the presence of officer whereby the affiant consciously takes upon himself the obligation of an oath and both the officer and the affiant must understand that an oath is being administered and taken. Bauknight v. State, 24 S.E.2d 217, 219, 68 Ga.App. 813.

In making affidavit that realty was not encumbered when application was made for loan by one charged with false swearing, it was immaterial that he allegedly did not hold up his hand in swearing, since it was not necessary for him to do so to make his act an "oath." Code 1933, § 26-4003. Brooks v. State, 11 S.E.2d 688, 690, 63 Ga.App. 575.

Oaths to affidavits ordinarily are not required to be administered with any particular ceremony, but the affiant must perform some corporal act before the officer whereby he consciously takes on himself the obligation of an "oath." Brooks v. State, 11 S.E.2d 688, 690, 63 Ga.App. 575.

OATH AUTHORIZED BY A LAW OF THE UNITED STATES

Oath administered by Senate subcommittee on investigations was an "oath authorized by a law of the United States", within statute defining essential elements of perjury. U. S. v. Debrow, Miss., 74 S.Ct. 113, 115, 346 U.S. 374, 98 L.Ed. 92.

OATH OF ALLEGIANCE

An "oath of allegiance", in simple form, requires pledges to support and defend the principles or purposes of the organization involved and may require loyalty to, and defense of, the constitution and bylaws thereof. Huntamer v. Coe, 246 P.2d 489, 492, 40 Wash.2d 767.

the best of his ability. Huntamer v. Coe, Wash., 246 P.2d 489, 492.

OBEDIENCE ORDINANCE

"Obedience ordinance", making unlawful "any" failure or refusal to comply with any lawful order, signal or direction of a police officer, was inconsistent with "obedience statute" making unlawful "any willful" failure or refusal to comply with any lawful order of a police officer; and, consequently, such ordinance was void. State v. Pascale, 134 A.2d 149, 151, 86 R.I. 182.

OBEDIENCE STATUTE

"Obedience ordinance", making unlawful "any" failure or refusal to comply with any lawful order, signal or direction of a police officer, was inconsistent with "obedience statute" making unlawful "any willful" failure or refusal to comply with any lawful order of a police officer; and, consequently, such ordinance was void. State v. Pascale, 134 A.2d 149, 151, 86 R.I. 182.

OBESITY

"Obesity" is an excessive development or excessive storage of fat throughout the body. United States v. 62 Packages, More or Less, of Marmola Prescription Tablets, D.C.Wis., 48 F.Supp. 878, 885.

OBITER

Statements in opinions wherein courts indulged in generalities that had no actual bearing on issues involved were "obiter". Graham v. Jones, 3 So.2d 761, 774, 198 La. 507.

"Obiter" is correctly defined as that useless chatter of judges, indulged in for reasons known only to them, to be printed at public expense. United States v. Certain Land in City of St. Louis, D.C.Mo., 29 F.Supp. 92, 95.

In granting writ of mandate to compel execution of bonds for municipal bus lines, District Court of Appeal would not state whether petition by amicus curiæ for intervention, which had been denied upon general grounds without opinion, was sufficient, since to do so would be mere "obiter". City of Mill Valley v. Saxton, 106 P.2d 455, 458, 41 Cal.App.2d 290.

Where a judgment, which ordered county auditor to pay over certain fund due under a judgment against county to be applied in satisfaction of plaintiff's judgment, was reversed for nonjoinder of necessary parties, appellate court would not consider county's right to assert by counterclaim a right to the fund by virtue of unpaid taxes due, since any statement on such issue would be mere "obiter". Lloyd v. Los Angeles County, 107 P.2d 622, 624, 41 Cal.App.2d 808.

Where specific question as to whether it is sufficient for party excepting to auditor's findings in equity case to point out where evidence relied on may be found by reference in excep-

Exhibit 15: A sample page from *Words and Phrases.*

CASE CITATORS

Shepard's Citations, the most comprehensive system of law citators, consists of a series of citation indexes for every state, every regional unit of the *National Reporter System,* the federal reports, the U. S. Supreme Court reports and even some reports of administrative agencies. These citation indexes are kept up to date with pamphlet supplementation on a regular basis. *Shepard's* lists the citation of virtually every published decision and then cites every later case which has cited that decision. It thereby provides a complete citation record of all appellate decisions, including leading periodical articles and attorney general opinions which have discussed those decisions. One never begins his research in *Shepard's,* however, but comes to it only with a citation to a primary authority whose status or history is sought.

Shepard's citators thus provide a unique and sophisticated method of accomplishing the following three purposes:

1. Tracing the judicial history of each case appearing in an official or West reporter, including parallel citations to that

case in the other reporter (as shown above in Exhibits 9 and 10) and citations to all later proceedings in that same case.

2.   Verifying the current status of each case in order to establish whether it is still effective law, or has been reversed, overruled, or its authority otherwise diminished.

3.   Finding later cases which have cited the main case, as well as developing research leads to periodical articles, attorney general opinions, etc.

As an example of how Shepard's handles a case, let us refer again to *Mallory vs. United States*, 354 U.S. 449 (1957).

To clarify the following explanations, Exhibit 16 below has been marked with letters to illustrate the various ways in which the cited case is treated. These different treatments include the following:

A—When the case is first listed in Shepard's, citations are given to the alternative *unofficial* reports of the *Mallory* case in *Supreme Court Reporter* and *Lawyers' Edition*. These citations appear in parentheses.

B—Next are listed the citations of the case in the U. S. Supreme Court and the lower federal courts, with appropriate

Vol. 354   UNITED STATES SUPREME

COURT REPORTS

—449—

A
(1 LE1479)
(77 SC1356)
s352 US 877
s 1 LE 79
s 77 SC 103

B
s236 F2d 701
s259 F2d 796
s259 F2d 801
p249 F2d 106
j280 F2d 610
285 F2d 677
202 FS 679
Arrest
Police Au-
thority–
Probable
Cause
164 FS 898
Crim. Law
Arraign-
ment–Delay

C
357 US 509
2 LE1528
78 SC1300
j362 US 250
j 4 LE 692
j 80 SC 703
j365 US 765
j 6 LE 81
j 81 SC 885
e367 US 585
e 6 LE1048
e 81 SC1869
248 F2d 655
d249 F2d 235
d250 F2d 31
j250 F2d 33
252 F2d 400
f252 F2d 614
252 F2d 854
d253 F2d 337
254 F2d 84
j254 F2d 765
d256 F2d 127
d256 F2d 280
e256 F2d 296
256 F2d 709
d257 F2d 176
d257 F2d 185

–Mas–
226NE208
371Mch604
124NW764
374Mch591
132NW679
3McA125
141NW663
6McA54
148NW216
150NW521
230Md 619
185A2d 367
231Md 489

D
191A2d 228
231Md 496
191A2d 232
234Md444
199A2d779
270Min338
133NW831
251Mis778
171So2d320
–Mis–
187So2d31

–Mo–
403SW605
146Mt235
405P2d766

–Nev–
428P2d378
39NJ 171
188A2d 18
43NJ167
203A2d11
43NJ593
206A2d748
49ABA438
49ABA555
51ABA439

E
51ABA466
51ABA827
52ABA444
53ABA427
34FRD170
34FRD198

F
40FRD356
16LE1298n
9A3899n
10A31057n

Exhibit 16:   The *Mallory* case as it appears in *Shepard's U. S. Citations.*

symbols to show the history of the *Mallory* case in its earlier stages.

C—Then follow citations to other decisions in the U. S. Supreme Court and the lower federal courts analyzed as to the treatment accorded the *Mallory* case in those cases. Symbols, such as "e" for explained, "d" for distinguished, or "f" for followed, indicate the nature of the citing court's treatment of the *Mallory* case. Explanations of all of the symbols so used are set forth in Exhibit 17 below. The subject matter involved in any particular point of law dealt with in this case is indicated by topic words under which are shown any citing references by the federal courts relating to that particular point of law. Thus, Criminal law–Arraignment–Delay indicates the subject matter of a point of law dealt with in the *Mallory* case which is also treated by the decision reported at 357 U.S. 509 and by the other cases listed thereunder. Through the topic word, the citations dealing with a particular point of law may be found instantly without examining every citation to the *Mallory* case.

D—This section lists citations to decisions in state reporters and units of the *Na-*

tional Reporter System arranged alphabetically by the state.

E—We find here that the *Mallory* case has been cited in periodical articles, such as the *American Bar Association Journal.*

F—The last section gives citations to articles and annotations where the *Mallory* case was cited in *Federal Rules Decisions* and annotated reporters, such as *Lawyers' Edition* and *A.L.R.*

ABBREVIATIONS—ANALYSIS

History of Case

a	(affirmed)	Same case affirmed on rehearing.
cc	(connected case)	Different case from case cited but arising out of same subject matter or intimately connected therewith.
m	(modified)	Same case modified on rehearing.
r	(reversed)	Same case reversed on rehearing.
s	(same case)	Same case as case cited.
S	(superseded)	Substitution for former opinion.
v	(vacated)	Same case vacated.
US reh den		Rehearing denied by U. S. Supreme Court.
US reh dis		Rehearing dismissed by U. S. Supreme Court.

Treatment of Case

c	(criticised)	Soundness of decision or reasoning in cited case criticised for reasons given.
d	(distinguished)	Case at bar different either in law or fact from case cited for reasons given.
e	(explained)	Statement of import of decision in cited case. Not merely a restatement of the facts.
f	(followed)	Cited as controlling.
h	(harmonized)	Apparent inconsistency explained and shown not to exist.
j	(dissenting opinion)	Citation in dissenting opinion.
L	(limited)	Refusal to extend decision of cited case beyond precise issues involved.
o	(overruled)	Ruling in cited case expressly overruled.
p	(parallel)	Citing case substantially alike or on all fours with cited case in its law or facts.
q	(questioned)	Soundness of decision or reasoning in cited case questioned.

NOTES

Absence from any bound volume or cumulative supplement of a reference to any United States Supreme Court case indicates that the case has not been cited within the scope of that volume or cumulative supplement.

Where the reports of more than one case start on the same page of any volume of reports, Shepard's United States Citations, Case Edition refers to the cases as "Case 1", "Case 2", etc. and shows the citations to each case accordingly.

Where the reports of more than one memorandum decision start on the same page of any volume of reports, Shepard's United States Citations, Case Edition refers to the decisions as "No. 55", "No. 349", etc. and shows the citations to each decision accordingly.

A reference enclosed in parentheses immediately following a reference to a case indicates a cross reference to another report of the same case.

Topic words do not apply to citations appearing below separation lines.

A letter "n" to the right of a citing page number indicates a citation in an annotation. Only the first citation of a case in an annotation or subdivision thereof is shown. A letter "s" to the right of a page number indicates a citation in a supplement to an annotation commencing on that page.

Exhibit 17: *Shepard's* Case Symbols with explanatory notes.

CHAPTER IV

STATUTES

Statutory material appears very early in recorded history, as evidenced by the legal codes of the ancient Near East, many of which are well known to us today (e. g. those of the Assyrians, Babylonians, Hittites, and particularly the Hebrew codes of the Bible). Legal codes were used throughout the ages to formulate new rules of kings or priests, as well as to codify existing custom and judicial pronouncements. There are fundamental differences between the decisional material of case law and the directive texts of statutory enactments: differences of purpose and source, of language and style, and of bibliographic form and reference.

There are also very significant differences between the statutory forms of different ages and legal systems. In modern times, Anglo-American laws have developed very differently from the Napoleonic codes in Europe. The Continental codes legislate in general terms, using provisions which are quite broad and yet concise and simple in language. American statutes, on the other hand, have sought to meet every future situation specifically, using many words and considerable detail to do so. The multiplicity of American statutes is in part due to our optimistic striving for a solution of all social and economic problems by legislation; the prolixity results from our desire to anticipate every conceivable violation. Although our compilations are often called codes, they are as different from the European codes as the Penal Law of Pennsylvania is from the Ten Commandments.

American and English statutes are published *chronologically* in separate volumes for each legislative year or session of the legislature. This chronological form of publication, like that of case reports, gives rise to the need for some means of subject access. The lawyer must find all the law which is currently applicable to his particular problem. Such an approach is provided by statutory compilations in which the laws *in force* are arranged by broad topics. Each such grouping is given a descriptive title and divided into numbered sections. A more or less detailed index enables the researcher to find the sections dealing with his particular problem or topic. These compilations (usually in an unofficial edition) will often include annotations to relevant court decisions from the same jurisdiction, which interpret, construe or apply each statutory section. Such annotations consist of a one sentence squib of the applicable legal principle and a citation to the case from which it was taken, just like the West headnote and digest summaries.

Statutory compilations must be updated promptly to include the output of the latest legislative session. Because of the numerous changes which are made in statutory law every time a legislature meets and because of the frequency of legislative sessions in this country (in 1969, 26 state legislatures were meeting annually and 24 biennially), it is necessary to provide some form of prompt and convenient supplementation. Failure to do so would render a legislative compilation virtually useless. Supplementation is usually provided by pocket parts in the back of the bound volumes or by looseleaf additions. Some official codes are updated only by the publication of revised editions every few years.

With statutes, as with case law, there are both official and unofficial editions and the *unofficial* texts usually provide additional research material which make them more useful than the official edition. For example, most of the *annotated* editions of statutes are published unofficially by commercial publishers. These usually provide faster and more convenient supplementation than the official editions, fuller editorial notes, his-

torical comments, analyses of statutes, and
other interpretative material. However, the
official text is, as always, the authoritative
one and must be cited in every legal reference.

The citation problem for statutes is somewhat complicated by the fact that there may
be *two* official sources: the *chronologically*
published session laws and a *subject* compilation of statutes in force. Usually only one
of these forms is the *authoritative* text, although both may be official. While the session law is generally the authoritative text,
the researcher may have difficulty in determining this. In a few states unofficial subject compilations have been recognized as
authoritative to some extent or for some purpose, because of the absence of convenient
official editions.

There are also jurisdictional problems of
statutory coverage and authority which
arise in part from our federal system and in
part from the multiplicity of state laws. We
have both a federal legislature and 50 state
legislatures. Sometimes there is conflict
between enactments of the United States
Congress and those of the states and sometimes uncertainty as to which law applies
in a particular situation. There are also
problems of interpretation and application

arising from the variety of laws on the same subject in the 50 states. This has given rise to a movement for uniform state laws, which is reflected in the work of the National Conference of Commissioners on Uniform State Laws.

It is also relevant to note that legislation comes not only from traditional legislative bodies like the Congress and the state legislatures, but also from subordinate legislative units. These other law-making bodies include administrative agencies and executive departments; courts which issue their own rules; towns, municipalities and other local units of government.

The nature of legal authority assigned to legislation is different from that of case law. Statutes have binding or mandatory authority in the jurisdiction in which they are enacted or promulgated. Outside of that jurisdiction they have no effect and are not even persuasive authority, except of course as evidence of the law of the state which enacted them. If, however, a state is contemplating the adoption of a law already passed by another state, the latter's experience under that law may be persuasive to the deliberating legislature or to later courts which may have to construe the statute.

Finally, it should be pointed out that our statutes are often marked by ambiguities or vagueness which give rise to legal controversy by making their interpretation and application difficult. This has led to a considerable concern with ascertaining the lawmakers' intent through the collection and study of documents of legislative history. This statutory ambiguity may stem from linguistic uncertainty or poor draftsmanship, but frequently is the inevitable result of negotiation and compromise in our legislative process.

TYPES OF LEGISLATION

We have already mentioned these different categories of legislative material:

1. Conventional legislation and subordinate or delegated legislation.

2. Federal and state legislation.

3. Statutory compilations and session laws.

4. Official and unofficial publications.

5. Authoritative and non-authoritative texts.

6. Annotated and unannotated editions.

There are other descriptive categories of legislation which should be mentioned.

Among them are the following forms which legislation can take in this country:

1. Constitutions are the organic laws of particular jurisdictions. They define political relationships; enumerate the rights and liberties of citizens; and create the necessary governmental framework. Constitutions are published in the statutory compilation of each jurisdiction, as well as in separate editions.

2. Resolutions (joint, concurrent and simple) and **Acts** are the forms by which a legislature carries on its work and promulgates laws. In the United States Congress, laws in the usual sense are passed by either a *joint resolution* or an *act*. Simple and concurrent resolutions are used for expressing the sentiment or intent of Congress or for performing housekeeping functions short of actual legislation. A simple resolution is the action of one house of Congress, while a concurrent resolution stems from both houses.

3. Treaties are the instruments by which sovereign nations can act or agree to act with other nations. Treaties are considered a legislative form, but are discussed separately in Chapter VIII below.

4. Interstate Compacts are agreements between two or more states, which are legislative in nature and somewhat like treaties in form and effect. Compacts require the consent of Congress before the states can enter into them, so they often appear in both federal and state legislative publications.

5. Reorganization Plans are presidential proposals to reorganize executive agencies below the departmental level which are submitted to Congress pursuant to a general authorizing statute. If Congress does not veto the plan, it becomes law automatically in a reversal of the usual legislative process —that is, enactment by the President, subject to veto by the Congress, instead of vice versa.

6. Executive Legislation includes presidential proclamations, orders and messages, all of which belong more properly in the area of administrative law and will be discussed in Chapter VI below.

7. Administrative Regulations (substantive and procedural) consist of rules adopted by executive and regulatory agencies, pursuant to congressional authorization, which are clearly legislative in nature. These will also be discussed in detail in Chapter VI below.

8. Court Rules are enactments, usually by courts themselves or conferences of judges, for the regulation of proceedings in the courts.

9. Local Laws and Ordinances are delegated legislation in that the power to legislate has been delegated by the state legislature to some law-making agency of local government. Publication is generally very poor in this area, although a tremendous number of such laws are enacted regularly by municipalities and counties.

In addition to the foregoing legislative categories, the distinction between *public laws* and *private laws* must also be mentioned. Public laws are those which are designed to affect the general public, as distinguished from private laws which are passed to meet a special need of an individual or small group. In some cases, the distinction is hard to justify, as when some special interest group gets legislation passed, which, although general in tone, actually affects very few people. Both types are passed in the same way and both usually appear in the session law publication, but only *public* laws become part of the compiled statutes.

The final important distinction between legislative forms concerns the three main classes of their publication: slip laws, session laws and subject compilations.

The *slip law* is the first published official text of a statute and is issued in a pamphlet or single sheet, usually separately paginated. Slip laws of the United States Congress are available shortly after enactment, but on the state level are often quite difficult to obtain.

The *session laws* are the next official form in which a statute appears. They consist of a chronological accumulation of slip laws, bound in one or more volumes and issued for a particular legislative session (hence the name). The session laws supersede the slip laws as the official statutory text and in most jurisdictions remain the authoritative text, only rarely being superseded for that purpose by the code or subject compilation. In federal law, the official session laws are the *U. S. Statutes at Large,* which is still the authoritative (or positive law) text of approximately two-thirds of the public laws. With respect to the other one-third, the *U. S. Code* (the federal subject compilation) has become the authoritative text. Those titles of the Code which have been reenacted as positive law and thus become authoritative are listed in the preface to each volume of the Code. Every state also has a session law form of some kind which is its official, chronological method of publication.

Subject compilations include the *current* text of all permanent *public* laws in force.

They consist of a topical arrangement under broad subjects, with an index, offering the researcher *subject access* to the otherwise chronologically published statutes. In most states the subject compilation is an unofficial edition, but some states have both an official compilation and an unofficial one. As noted above, the unofficial edition is usually preferred by researchers because very often it will contain annotations to court decisions, useful editorial notes, and better supplementation than the official text. Subject compilations must, of course, be kept up to date to reflect the latest legislative changes and this is usually done by annual pocket parts, although a few states use looseleaf sheets.

FEDERAL STATUTORY FORMS

1. **The Quick Text.** Many laws take effect upon enactment or soon thereafter and, whether immediately effective or not, lawyers and researchers want to have the text of such new laws as soon as possible. One source is the newspaper report of the passage or signing of important laws. In well documented papers like the *New York Times,* the law may appear in full text. Longer or less newsworthy acts, however, will rarely be

reproduced in full even there. Congress itself is the best source for the text of new
laws immediately after enactment.

As we have seen, the first *official* text is
the *slip law,* which can be requested from
the appropriate congressional clerk or an individual congressman, or ordered from the
Superintendent of Documents, U. S. Government Printing Office, on an individual basis
or by subscription. There is often, however,
a frustrating time lag between enactment
and distribution of slip laws.

Commercially published specialized loose-
leaf services provide a quick text of federal
enactments in particular subject fields.
Since these publications are usually supplemented on a weekly basis, they are an excellent source for new legislation. Such
services are commonly published in public
law fields like taxation, labor law, trade regulation, etc. and will be discussed below in
Chapter VII. Their publishers will also frequently supply copies of new laws at the
request of subscribers, even though they do
not appear in full in the service itself.

One of the most popular sources of new
federal *public* laws is the *U. S. Code Congressional and Administrative News,* pub-

lished fortnightly by West during the congressional session and monthly when Congress is not in session. It appears initially in an advance sheet edition containing the complete text of all public laws along with some legislative history (in the form of committee reports) on the more important enactments. *U.S.C.C.A.N.* also contains congressional news notes, selected administrative regulations, executive documents, and rather useful tables and indexes.

2. Session Law Form. At the end of each session of Congress, the public and private slip laws are accumulated, corrected and issued in bound volumes as the official *Statutes at Large* for that session. These are cited by volume and page, for example, 72 Stat. 962 (referring to volume 72 of the *Statutes at Large,* page 962). The *Statutes at Large* supersede the slip laws as the authoritative text of federal laws and remain the authoritative text for all but those 19 titles of the *U. S. Code* which have been reenacted as positive law. The *Statutes at Large* contain an index for each session, but since these indexes do not cumulate the researcher must use the topical arrangement of the *U. S. Code* and *its* general index in order to locate the current law on a particular subject.   The following exhibit shows a brief statute in the *Statutes at Large:*

Public Law 89-335

November 8, 1965
[H. R. 5493]

Lexington, Mass., Display of U.S. flag.

56 Stat. 1074.

AN ACT

To provide that the flag of the United States of America may be flown for twenty-four hours of each day in Lexington, Massachusetts.

Be it enacted by the Senate and House of Representatives of the United States of America in Congress assembled, That, notwithstanding any rule or custom pertaining to the display of the flag of the United States of America as set forth in the joint resolution entitled "Joint resolution to codify and emphasize existing rules and customs pertaining to the display and use of the flag of the United States of America", approved June 22, 1942 (36 U.S.C. 171–178), the flag of the United States of America may be flown for twenty-four hours of each day on the green of the town of Lexington, Massachusetts.   The flag may not be flown pursuant to the authority contained in this Act during the hours from sunset to sunrise unless it is illuminated.

Approved November 8, 1965.

Exhibit 18:   *The Statutes at Large.*

There are also two unofficial session law texts of public laws.   *U. S. Code Congressional and Administrative News,* mentioned above, is published by the West Publishing Company separately and as a supplement to its United States Code Annotated. Issued initially during each congressional session in advance sheets, *U.S.C.C.A.N.* cumulates at the end of each session into bound volumes which provide a permanent record of public legislation with a selection of legislative history in the form of congressional committee reports.

Federal Code Annotated, published by Lawyers Coop, is another subject compilation of federal statutes. It is supplemented by a service called *Current Public Laws and Administrative Material,* which provides the texts of public laws, first in advance sheets and then in an annual bound volume. These provide subscribers to the *F.C.A.* with a session law service similar to that of *U.S.C.C. A.N.,* but without legislative history. Neither *U.S.C.C.A.N.* nor *Current Public Laws and Administrative Material* include *private* laws; these are only available in the official *Statutes at Large.*

3. Subject Compilations. Since federal laws are published initially in the chronological *Statutes at Large,* some means of subject access is necessary. Without such access, attorneys and scholars who seek laws on a particular topic would have the impossible task of searching the separate indexes of every volume of session laws. Even then they could not be sure that a relevant law had not been amended or repealed in a later volume.

The first official subject compilations designed to provide such access were the *U. S. Revised Statutes* of 1873 and its second edition of 1878. These one volume compilations arranged all *public, general* and *permanent* federal statutes into some 75 titles or subject categories with consecutive section numbering and a general index. The *Revised Statutes* of 1873 was more than just a subject compilation, however. It actually reenacted as positive law the statutes it contained and expressly repealed their original *Statutes at Large* texts. Therefore, for those public laws which predate 1873 and are included in the *Revised Statutes*, that compilation has become their authoritative text. The second edition, however, did not have that status, although little distinction is made between them today.

Although it soon became apparent that the *Revised Statutes* were not adequate to provide a convenient subject arrangement of current federal statutes, no other official compilation was prepared for almost fifty years. Then in 1926, the first edition of the *United States Code* was published, arranging the public, general, permanent laws by subject into some 50 titles. The Code is published in a completely revised edition every 6 years with bound cumulative supplements in the intervening years. As previously noted, the statutes contained in approximately one-third of the titles of the Code have been *reenacted* and for them the Code has become the authoritative text. For the others, the *Statutes at Large* retain that status. The congressional plan of reenactment is described in the preface of the Code as follows:

"Inasmuch as many of the general and permanent laws which are required to be incorporated in this Code are inconsistent, redundant, and obsolete, the Committee on the Judiciary is engaged in a comprehensive project of revising and enacting the Code into law, title by title. In furtherance of this plan bills have been enacted to revise, codify and enact into law Titles 1, 3, 4, 6, 9, 10, 13, 14, 17, 18, 23, 28, 32, 35, 37, 38, 39. In addition, bills relating to other titles are being prepared for introduction at an early date. When this work is completed all the titles of the Code will be legal evidence of the general and permanent law and recourse to the numerous

[*83*]

volumes of the Statutes at Large for this purpose will be unnecessary."

Titles 5 and 44 were similarly reenacted after this preface appeared.

Citations to the Code refer to title and section, rather than to volume and page as in the *Statutes at Large.* For example, 18 U.S.C. § 1621 describes Title 18 of the *U. S. Code,* section 1621. If the title is one of those reenacted into positive law, it is technically unnecessary to cite its *Statutes at Large* source, but the general practice is to do so.

In addition to the actual text of statutes, the Code also includes historical and editorial notes, parallel tables and other research aids. Each section of the Code is followed by citation to the *Statutes at Large* provision which originally enacted it. These alternative citations are particularly important where the *Statutes at Large* is still the authoritative source and must be cited. This and other features of the *U. S. Code* are illustrated in Exhibit 19.

Designation in said section 421 of title 18, U. S. C., 1940 ed., of offender as a "pirate" was omitted as unnecessary. The punishment provision of section 1582 of this title (incorporated by reference in said section 425) has been adopted as consistent with other slave-trade statutes rather than the life-imprisonment penalty contained in said sections 421 and 422 of title 18, U. S. C., 1940 ed. However, the requirement in section 1582 of this title that one-half the fine be for the "use of the person prosecuting the indictment to effect" was omitted as meaningless.

Mandatory-punishment provisions were rephrased in the alternative. (See reviser's note under section 201 of this title.)

CROSS REFERENCES

Slavery abolished, see Const. Amend. 13.

§ 1586. Service on vessels in slave trade.

Whoever, being a citizen or resident of the United States, voluntarily serves on board of any vessel employed or made use of in the transportation of slaves from any foreign country or place to another, shall be fined not more than $2,000 or imprisoned not more than two years, or both. (June 25, 1948, ch. 645, 62 Stat. 773.)

LEGISLATIVE HISTORY

Reviser's Note.—Based on title 18, U. S. C., 1940 ed., § 427 (Mar. 4, 1909, ch. 321, § 252, 35 Stat. 1139.)

Mandatory-punishment provisions were rephrased in the alternative. (See reviser's note under section 201 of this title.)

CROSS REFERENCES

Slavery abolished, see Const. Amend. 13.

§ 1587. Possession of slaves aboard vessel.

Whoever, being the captain, master, or commander of any vessel found in any river, port, bay, harbor, or on the high seas within the jurisdiction of the United States, or hovering off the coast thereof, and having on board any person for the purpose of selling such person as a slave, or with intent to land such person for such purpose, shall be fined not more than $10,000 or imprisoned not more than four years, or both. (June 25, 1948, ch. 645, 62 Stat. 773.)

tuted, in view of section 5 of this title defining "United States".

CROSS REFERENCES

Slavery abolished, see Const. Amend. 13.

Chapter 79.—PERJURY

Sec.
1621. Perjury generally.
1622. Subornation of perjury.

§ 1621. Perjury generally.

Whoever, having taken an oath before a competent tribunal, officer, or person, in any case in which a law of the United States authorizes an oath to be administered, that he will testify, declare, depose, or certify truly, or that any written testimony, declaration, deposition, or certificate by him subscribed, is true, willfully and contrary to such oath states or subscribes any material matter which he does not believe to be true, is guilty of perjury, and shall, except as otherwise expressly provided by law, be fined not more than $2,000 or imprisoned not more than five years, or both. (June 25, 1948, ch. 645, 62 Stat. 773.)

LEGISLATIVE HISTORY

Reviser's Note.—Based on title 18, U. S. C., 1940 ed., §§ 231, 629 (Mar. 4, 1909, ch. 321, § 125, 35 Stat. 1111; June 15, 1917, ch. 30, title XI, § 19, 40 Stat. 230).

Words "except as otherwise expressly provided by law" were inserted to avoid conflict with perjury provisions in other titles where the punishment and application vary.

More than 25 additional provisions are in the code. For construction and application of several such sections, see Behrle v. United States (App. D. C. 1938, 100 F. 2d 714), United States v. Hammer (D. C. N. Y., 1924, 299 F. 1011, affirmed, 6 F. 2d 786), Rosenthal v. United States (1918, 248 F. 684, 160 C. C. A. 584), cf. Epstein v. United States (1912, 196 F. 354, 116 C. C. A. 174, certiorari denied 32 S. Ct. 527, 223 U. S. 731, 56 L. ed. 634).

Mandatory-punishment provisions were rephrased in the alternative. (See reviser's note under section 201 of this title.)

Minor verbal changes were made.

CANAL ZONE

Applicability of section to Canal Zone, see section 14 of this title.

Exhibit 19: A page in Title 18 of the official *United States Code.*

In order to get from the *Statutes at Large* citation to the Code citation, tables are provided at the end of the *U. S. Code* itself, which give such parallel references. The form of these tables, as revised in the 1964 edition of the Code, is shown in Exhibit 20.

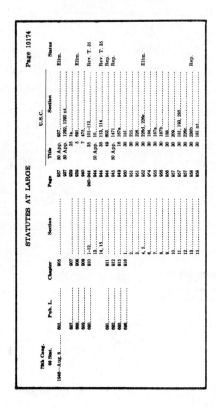

Exhibit 20: A parallel reference table in the latest edition of the *U. S. Code.*

4. Annotated Subject Compilations. In addition to the *U. S. Code,* which is the official subject compilation, there are also two privately published, annotated editions of the Code. As noted above, these are the *U. S. Code Annotated (U.S.C.A.)* published by West and the *Federal Code Annotated (F.C.A.)* published by Lawyers Coop. Both compilations follow the same title and section numbering as the official edition and contain the same statutory text, but add the following features:

(a) Annotations of court decisions, interpreting, construing, and applying each section.

(b) Editorial notes and analytical discussions on particular statutes or provisions.

(c) References to attorney general opinions and legislative history.

(d) Supplementation by annual pocket parts, quarterly pamphlets, and revised volumes as necessary.

F.C.A. also preserves the original *Statutes at Large* context in which the statute was enacted, while both the *U.S.C.* and *U.S.C.A.* may make minor changes in integrating particular provisions into the Code format.

Their special research aids have made the annotated statutes very popular with attorneys and scholars and they are therefore used widely in preference to the official text. Exhibit 21 shows the *U.S.C.A.* version of the same section of Title 18 as was shown in Exhibit 19. Exhibit 22 shows a page of annotations to court decisions following that section in *U.S.C.A.*; it also illustrates the summary indexing of such annotations.

CHAPTER 79—PERJURY

Sec.
1621. Perjury generally.
1622. Subornation of perjury.

§ 1621. Perjury generally

Whoever, having taken an oath before a competent tribunal, officer, or person, in any case in which a law of the United States authorizes an oath to be administered, that he will testify, declare, depose, or certify truly, or that any written testimony, declaration, deposition, or certificate by him subscribed, is true, willfully and contrary to such oath states or subscribes any material matter which he does not believe to be true, is guilty of perjury, and shall, except as otherwise expressly provided by law, be fined not more than $2,000 or imprisoned not more than five years, or both. June 25, 1948, c. 645, 62 Stat. 773.

Historical and Revision Notes

Reviser's Note. Based on Title 18, U.S.C., 1940 ed., §§ 231, 629 (Mar. 4, 1909, c. 321, § 125, 35 Stat. 1111 [Derived from R. S. § 5392]; June 15, 1917, c. 30, Title XI, § 19, 40 Stat. 230).

Words "except as otherwise expressly provided by law" were inserted to avoid conflict with perjury provisions in other titles where the punishment and application vary.

N.Y.1924, 299 F. 1011, affirmed, 6 F.2d 786), Rosenthal v. United States (1918, 248 F. 684, 160 C.C.A. 584), cf. Epstein v. United States (1912, 196 F. 354, 116 C.C. A. 174, certiorari denied 32 S.Ct. 527, 223 U.S. 731, 56 L.Ed. 634).

Mandatory-punishment provisions were rephrased in the alternative. (See reviser's note under section 201 of this title.)

Minor verbal changes were made. 80th

Exhibit 21: The *United States Code Annotated:* 18 U.S.C.A. § 1621.

5. Constitutional Texts and Sources. The United States Constitution appears in numerous publications ranging from simple pamphlets put out by patriotic organizations to large annotated texts with full scholarly apparatus. It is also included in most subject compilations of federal and state statutes. The best separate edition had been that edited by Edward Corwin and published by the Library of Congress in 1953. A revised edition of this work by Lester Jayson was pub-

---

Tit. 18, § 1621
Note 1

CRIMES

Ch. 79

I. GENERALLY

Subdivision Index

---

1. Historical

"This statute [former section 231 of this title] takes the place of the similar provision of § 5392 of the Revised Statutes, which in turn was a substitute for a number of statutes in regard to perjury, and was phrased so as to embrace all cases of false swearing, whether in a court of justice or before administrative officers acting within their powers." U. S. v. Smull, Or.1915, 35 S.Ct. 349, 236 U.S. 405, 59 L.Ed. 641.

2. Effective date

Act March 3, 1825, c. 65, 4 Stat. 118, in relation to perjury, being a general law, applied to all subsequent cases which came within it. U. S. v. Nihols, C.C. Mich.1845, Fed.Cas.No.15,880.

court more severely than in any other Federal District Court. O'Brien v. U. S., 1938, 99 F.2d 368, 69 App.D.C. 135, certiorari denied 59 S.Ct. 95, 305 U.S. 562, 83 L.Ed. 354.

5. Territorial limits of section

Former section 231 of this title was of universal application within the territorial limits of the United States, and was not limited to those portions which were within the exclusive jurisdiction of the national government. Caha v. U. S., Kan.1894, 14 S.Ct. 513, 152 U.S. 211, 38 L.Ed. 415.

6. Definition of case

A false statement on oath concerning his property, made by a person justifying as surety on a bail bond, came within the meaning of the word "case" used in former section 231 of this title. U. S. v. Voltz, C.C.N.Y.1876, 14 Blatchf. 15, 28 Fed.Cas.No.16,627.

An indictment for an act which did not constitute an offense under the laws of the United States was still "a suit, controversy, matter or cause pending," in which perjury might be committed under Act Apr. 3, 1790, c. 9, 1 Stat. 116. U. S. v. Reese, C.C.1866, Fed.Cas.No.16,138, reversed on another ground 9 Wall. 13, 19 L.Ed. 541.

7. Time of commission

The truth or falsity of testimony of

Exhibit 22: Annotations to 18 *U.S.C.A.* § 1621.

lished in 1964 with the title: *The Constitution of the United States of America, Analysis and Interpretation.* It includes the text of the Constitution along with case annotations and detailed discussions of each provision, its history and interpretation. Unless regularly supplemented, however, this edition will shortly suffer the same premature obsolescence as its predecessor. A new edition has been announced for publication at the end of 1972.

The Constitution appears in the *U. S. Code,* the *U.S.C.A.* and the *F.C.A.,* although it is not an integral part of the Code itself. Probably the most useful and most popular text of the Constitution is that appearing in six volumes in the *U.S.C.A.* where it is heavily annotated with thousands of case abstracts.

There is also a great historical literature concerning the original drafting and adoption of the Constitution. Among the most useful of these publications are *Documents Illustrative of the Formation of the Union of American States* (U.S.G.P.O.1927); *Documentary History of the Constitution of the U.S.A., 1786–1870* (U.S.Dept. of State, 1894–1905) in five volumes; and Max Farrand's *Records of the Federal Convention of 1787* in four volumes (Yale Univ. Press 1937, reprinted in paperback 1967).

6. Other Statutory Sources. Looseleaf services which collect legal source material in certain subject areas and are kept up-to-date by weekly supplementation, offer another practical means of access to statutes, as noted above. There are also subject compilations of statutes put out by various groups in the areas of their interest. These include *government agencies* (e. g. *Federal Labor Laws and Agencies,* issued by the Department of Labor); *Congress* itself (e. g. *Radio Laws of the U. S.* and *Laws Relating to Veterans*); *trade associations* (e. g. *Credit Manual of Commercial Laws,* published by the National Association of Credit Men); and *private publishers* (e. g. Schneider's *Workmen's Compensation Laws*). These collections are often quite helpful to people working in fields of law which are not serviced by looseleaf publications. However, they are never kept up-to-date with the same regularity as looseleaf services (in fact many are never supplemented at all) and thus must be used with considerable caution and updated by some other means.

STATE STATUTES

Most of the significant forms encountered in federal statutes also appear in state statutes. There are official and unofficial editions of state statutes; annotated and unannotated texts; slip laws, session laws, and subject compilations; acts and resolutions; public and private laws. There are also the universal problems of providing for subject access to chronologically published laws and keeping up-to-date an ever-changing mass of legislation. In fact, the publication of state laws reproduces many of the achievements, difficulties and short-comings of federal statutory publication.

1. State Constitutions. State constitutions have developed a bibliography of their own because of their variety and legal importance. There is an excellent looseleaf

---

CIVIL RIGHTS

See ALIENS; CIVIL SERVICE — IN-SERVICE PROVISIONS — DISCRIMINATION; CITIZENSHIP; COLORED PERSONS; EDUCATION — PUBLIC SCHOOLS—SEGREGATION; ELECTIONS —QUALIFICATIONS OF ELECTORS—RACIAL; PUBLIC OFFICERS — QUALIFICATIONS — RACIAL; PARKS AND RECREATION — RACIAL SEGREGATION; WOMEN; RELIGION — DISCRIMINATION;—FREEDOM OF OPINION AND CONSCIENCE.

All persons equal and entitled to equal rights, opportunities and protection under law; all persons have corresponding obligations to people and state. **Alas I 1.**

No person to be denied enjoyment of civil or political rights because of race, color, creed or national origin. **Alas I 3.**

Right of all persons to fair and just treatment in course of executive investigations not to be infringed. **Alas I 7.**

No citizen to be deprived of right, privilege or immunity, or exempted from burden or duty on account of race, color, or previous condition of servitude. **Ark II 3.**

No person to be denied enjoyment of civil rights or be discriminated against because of race, religion, sex or ancestry. **H I 4.**

Exhibit 23: An entry in the *Index-Digest of State Constitutions.*

compilation of state constitutions called *Constitutions of the U. S.: National and State* (Oceana, 1962) in two volumes, and a companion volume, the *Index-Digest of State Constitutions* (Columbia University Legislative Drafting Research Fund, 2nd ed. 1959), which provides subject access to all of the constitutions.

The best sources for individual state constitutions, however, are still the annotated statutes of the individual states, where one can usually find the latest text of the constitution, along with annotations of court decisions interpreting and construing it. Popular pamphlet texts are also available in many states. *Shepard's Citations* for the various states are useful in developing both legislative and judicial histories of state constitutions.

2. **State Session Laws.** Slip laws are issued in many of the states, but are rarely distributed to the public. However, every state has a session law publication which cumulates on a chronological basis the laws enacted at each sitting of its legislature. The names of the official state session laws vary from state to state (e. g. *Laws of New York, Acts and Resolves of Massachusetts*, etc.), but every state has some publication of this type, usually with a non-cumulative index for each volume or session. These chrono-

logical collections are similar to the *U. S. Statutes at Large* in form and purpose. They are initially the authoritative text of each state's laws and in most states never lose that status, since only rarely does the subject compilation acquire positive law status. In citing session laws, one must always include the year of the session, e. g. *Laws of New York, 1964.* Without the year, the citation is meaningless.

There is a considerable time lag in the publication of most state session laws and they are often delayed until long after the end of the session. In some states, the commercial publisher of the statutory compilation provides a "session law service" which gives access to new session laws even while the legislature is still sitting, very much as the *U. S. Code Congressional and Administrative News* and *Current Public Laws and Administrative Material* do for congressional enactments.

Several years ago the American Bar Foundation established a computer-produced subject index to current state statutes which is kept up-to-date by regular supplements. Originally called *Current State Legislation,* and then *Automated Statutory Reporter,* it is now published by the Aspen Systems Corporation under the title, *Computerized Law Index.* Exhibit 24 below shows part of a sample page which illustrates its key-word-in-context indexing method.

3. State Subject Compilations. Since the indexes to the state session laws do not cumulate, there is again need for some means of

to adopt any building.	**PLUMBING,** electrical, gas, or fir .... **Va**	**C 700**
tion for coal workers'	**PNEUMOCONIOSIS,** pulmonary emphyse .... **Ky**	**C 16**
or employment with the	**POLICE** or fire departments / excl .... **Ky**	**C 26**
applicants for fire or	**POLICE** forces / requires a minimu .... **Mass**	**C 162**
of 5 feet 7 inches for	**POLICE** force members. .... **Mass**	**C 162**
nd photographed by the	**POLICE.** .... **Mass**	**C 181**
applicants for fire or	**POLICE** service. .... **Mass**	**C 155**
Grants special	**POLICE** officer training powers to .... **Tenn**	**C 575**
Authorizes	**POLICE** authorities in any county .... **Va**	**C 611**
ations / establishes a	**POLICE** recruit training program a .... **Tenn**	**C 575**
g Commission and fixes	**POLICE** officer qualifications / e .... **Tenn**	**C 575**
as defense counsel for	**POLICE** and citizens who have part .... **Okla**	**S 393**
within which municipal	**POLICE** officers may make arrests. .... **S.C.**	**R 1354**
e of free licenses for	**POLICE** work dogs. .... **N.Y.**	**C 55**
s Long Island Railroad	**POLICE** as peace officers. .... **N.Y.**	**C 102**
the Capital Buildings	**POLICE** Force of the Office of Gen .... **N.Y.**	**C 205**
xecutive department as	**POLICE** officers. .... **N.Y.**	**C 205**
Authorizes the	**POLICE** Commissioner, upon applica .... **N.Y.**	**C 117**
ars of age / permits a	**POLICEMAN** to elect to have his re .... **Va**	**C 599**
	POLICEMAN'S Benefits: .... **Va**	**C 599**
s a month relief for a	**POLICEMAN'S** widow and 75 dollars .... **Va**	**C 599**
rport managers special	**POLICEMEN** / provides for licensin .... **Va**	**C 717**
Permits railroad	**POLICEMEN** to possess weapons. .... **N.Y.**	**C 13**
d makes provisions for	**POLICEMEN'S** and firemen's pension .... **Ky**	**C 26**
rry out the Governor's	**POLICIES** in the areas of public s .... **Md**	**C 401**
s concerning insurance	**POLICIES** / specifies violations a .... **Okla**	**H 1752**
from selling insurance	**POLICIES** to the state / provides .... **Tenn**	**C 567**
workmen's compensation	**POLICY** in the event that the insu .... **Va**	**C 766**
an official operating	**POLICY** pamphlet discribing their .... **Tenn**	**C 522**
States the Maryland	**POLICY** on mental hygiene and defi .... **Md**	**C 407**
Provides for a state	**POLICY** of preserving wetlands and .... **Md**	**C 241**
tantial benefit to the	**POLICYHOLDER.** .... **Md**	**C 428**
district to be a body	**POLITIC** and corporate / requires .... **Mass**	**C 150**
ublic corporation as a	**POLITICAL** subdivision for the pur .... **Ark**	**S 157**
ospitals Corporation a	**POLITICAL** subdivision for purpose .... **N.Y.**	**C 58**
regulations and grants	**POLITICAL** subdivisions contiguous .... **Va**	**C 196**

Exhibit 24: *Computerized Law Index*

subject access to relevant laws in force. Most states now have a subject compilation of their statutes, similar to the *U. S. Code,* which serves that function. These are usually commercially published, unofficial collections, which typically include annotations of court decisions on those statutes. For a few states, there is no unofficial edition and the state itself may publish an official subject compilation, usually without annotations. In a few other states, there is both an official and an unofficial edition of the code. As one might suspect, the better edited and more useful unofficial editions are gradually driving out the less elaborate (but usually less expensive) official sets.

The authority of the unofficial editions varies from state to state. It is usually accepted as at least *prima facie* evidence of the statutory law. They are rarely considered the "positive law" or authoritative text of statutes, but that distinction is becoming increasingly a matter of form rather than substance. One can usually determine the status of a subject compilation by looking for a certificate which indicates its authority in the front of each volume. Sometimes such information is supplied in the preface.

State statutes are annotated and supplemented in much the same way as federal statutes. The West Publishing Company's state codes are usually similar to *U.S.C.A.* in format and coverage. The best of them contain analytical notes, reference to historical sources, parallel tables, citations to attorney general opinions, and other useful research material, in addition to the usual judicial annotations. Supplementation is generally by pocket part or looseleaf insertions, although West also provides quarterly pamphlet supplements and session law services for most of its codes.

4. Uniform Laws. As noted above, there has been a movement in this country for some years to secure enactment by the states of various uniform laws. It has been felt that in many fields there is unnecessary confusion and conflict because of widely different state statutes. Sometimes this is a necessary reflection of the peculiar history, customs, economics or geography of the region, but in many cases there is no reasonable justification for these differences. The National Conference of Commissioners on the Uniform State Laws is a quasi-official body with representatives from every state, which meets annually to propose, draft, and promote uniform legislation. There are now over 75 such acts which have been passed by at least one state. Among the most

[*97*]

widely adopted is the *Uniform Commercial Code* which has been adopted by every state.

All of the uniform laws are compiled and published by West in one annotated set called *Uniform Laws Annotated* (Master edition, 1968–). Not only does this set contain every uniform law adopted by at least one state, along with the commissioners' notes on these laws, but it also includes annotations to the court decisions of *every* state which has adopted and then litigated each law. These annotations are particularly useful in giving enacting states the benefit of the case law developed in those states having the same uniform law. The *U.L.A.* also contains tables indicating which states have adopted each law, variations in their adoptions, and other useful information. The set is kept up-to-date annually by pocket parts and is supplemented by the annual *Handbooks of the National Conference of Commissioners on the Uniform State Laws* which provide current information about new laws, discussions of pending and proposed laws, and recent adoptions.

The text of each uniform law can, of course, also be found in the statutes of each state which has adopted that law, usually with annotations on the law from the courts of that particular state.

5. Procedural Legislation and Court Rules.

There are legal and bibliographic distinctions between procedural and substantive legislation. Procedural laws describe the procedures to be followed in the courts in effectuating one's legal rights and remedies. They concern the forms of action and defense, motion practice, time limitations, service of papers, hearing and trial arrangements, and all of the thousands of other details relating to the administration of legal business. In many states these procedural requirements are statutory in form, as in the Civil Practice Acts; in some states, they appear as non-statutory rules promulgated by the judiciary. In others, the procedural law is a combination of both statutes and rules.

Most statutory subject compilations include both substantive and procedural law, but in many states the procedural law is also separately published in unofficial services or manuals. These are typically annotated with court decisions and sometimes with sample forms to guide the practicing attorney. Such practice manuals are generally well supplemented or frequently revised.

Every state also has local court rules which govern the operation of their courts. These tend to be even more specific than the civil practice acts or rules, including such things as hours of court, make-up of court calendars, place and times for filing legal papers, etc. Court rules are published in the following forms: (a) as issued, in the official state reports (sometimes indicated by a notation on the spine of the particular volume that it contains new rules); (b) in the state statutory compilations; and (c) in separate pamphlets issued by the particular court.

6.　Local Law Sources. As we have seen, our legal system encompasses many different levels of jurisdiction—federal, state, county, town, city. Legislation is passed by all of these units and there is a large literature of local ordinances, charters, and codes, which is usually poorly published, rarely annotated and infrequently supplemented. Many of the larger cities in the United States now publish collections of their ordinances with some attempt at supplementation (e. g. Philadelphia Code of Ordinances, New York City Charter and Administrative Code, etc.), but for the rest, very little effort is made for proper publication. As some legal publishers begin to see the gold in those hills, more and more local law compilations are appearing. On the whole, however, the situation is still very bad and in many cities there is no accessible, up-to-date compilation of ordinances. The astute lawyer must familiarize himself with what is generally available in his area and then take steps to locate sources of further information.

FINDING-TOOLS FOR STATUTES

In addition to the subject compilations of statutes, there are other aids to statutory research. Among these are indexes of various kinds, which provide a direct topical approach to statutes, and tables which permit the researcher to convert citations from one form to another.

1. Indexes to Federal Statutes. Among the useful retrospective indexes to federal laws are Beaman and MacNamara, *Index Analysis of the Federal Statutes, 1789–1873* and McClenon and Gilbert, *Index to the Federal Statutes, 1874–1931.* The indexes to the *Revised Statutes* (1873 and 1878 editions) and to the various editions of the *U. S. Code* permit searching of those compilations as well.

There are indexes to current statutes by their legislative session in the volumes of the *Statutes at Large* and its unofficial editions described above. Indexes for entire body of currently effective federal statutes can be found in the *U. S. Code, U. S. Code*

Annotated and *Federal Code Annotated.*
These are probably the most frequently used
of all statutory indexes, since most research
is done in the latest subject compilations.
The section of the *U. S. Code* index shown
in Exhibit 25 below is typical of this group.

CIVIL RIGHTS—Continued

Actions or proceedings—Continued

    Deprivation of rights, 42 § 1983
        Form of action, 42 § 1983
        Persons liable, 42 § 1983
    Jurisdiction,
        District court, 28 §§ 1343, 1344; 42 § 1971
        Proceedings in vindication, 42 § 1988
    Removal of cases, 28 § 1443

Aliens, discrimination on account of being, 18 § 242

Armed forces, discrimination against person wearing
    uniform, 18 § 244

Arrests, fees, 42 § 1991

Attorney, assignment for defense in contempt cases, 42
    § 1971

Color,
    Discrimination or deprivation on account of, 18
        § 212
    Exclusion of jurors on account of, 18 § 243; 42
        § 1984

Color of law, deprivation of rights under, 18 § 242

Commission on Civil Rights, 42 §§ 1975–1975e

Exhibit 25: A section of the index
to the *United States
Code.*

For federal statutes which have become
commonly known by a popular name, there
are popular name tables (similar to those
described above for cases) which provide citations to their actual text. Such tables
can be found in the *Shepard's Acts and Cases
by Popular Names—Federal and State* which
replaced an earlier pamphlet form; in the
*Digest of the Supreme Court Reports: Table
of statutes by popular name*; and in the des-

ignated volumes of the *U.S.C., U.S.C.A.* and *F.C.A.* Exhibit 26 illustrates the Shepard's table:

Cor	FEDERAL AND STATE ACTS CITED BY POPULAR NAMES

Corrupt Practices Acts
U. S. Code 1964 Title 2, §241 et seq.
U. S. Code 1964 Title 18, §§591, 597, 599, 609, 610
Jan. 26, 1907, c. 420, 34 Stat. 864
June 25, 1910, c. 392, 36 Stat. 822
Oct. 16, 1918, c. 187, 40 Stat. 1013
Feb. 28, 1925, c. 368, §§301-319, 43 Stat. 1053
Ala. Code 1958, Title 17, §268 et seq.
Ark. Stat. 1947, 3-1301 et seq.
Colo. Rev. Stat. 1963, 49-23-2 et seq.
Conn. Gen. Stat. 1958, §9-333 et seq.
Fla. Stat. 1965, 99.161
Ill. Rev. Stat. 1965, Ch. 102, §1 et seq.
Ind. Burns' 1949 Repl., 29-5701 et seq.
Kan. Stat. Anno. 25-1701 et seq.
Ky. Rev. Stat. 1962, 123.010 et seq.
Mas. Gen. Laws 1932, Ch. 55
Md. Anno. Code 1957, Art. 33, §211 et seq.
Mich. Comp. Laws 1948, 168.901 et seq., 168.931 et seq.
Min. Stat. 1965, 211.01 et seq.

Cortland City Court Act
N. Y. Laws 1935, Ch. 423

Cosmetic Act
U. S. Code 1964 Title 21, §301 et seq.
June 25, 1938, c. 675, 52 Stat. 1040
Ark. Stat. 1947, 82-1101 et seq.
Cal. Health and Safety Code §26001 et seq.
Haw. Rev. Laws 1955, §51-1 et seq.
N. C. Gen. Stat. 1943, §106-120 et seq.
N. D. Century Code 19-09-01 et seq.
N. H. Rev. Stat. 1955, 146:1 et seq.
Wash. Rev. Code 1951, Ch. 69.04

Cosmetic and Drug Act
Ga. Code 1933, 42-1501 et seq.
N. M. Stat. Anno. 1953, 54 8-1 et seq.

Cosmetic and Hazardous Substance Labeling Act
Vt. Stat. Anno. 1959, Title 18, §4051 et seq.

<u>Exhibit 26</u>: The popular name tables for statutes in *Shepard's Acts and Cases by Popular Name.*

2. Parallel Conversion and Transfer Tables. In view of the varied forms which statutes take, it is necessary to provide parallel reference tables from one form or stage of a law to another form or a later stage of the same law. The following is a list of the most commonly used tables or aids and where they can be found:

(a) **Bill number to public law number:**

(1) In legislative status tables which include enactments (e. g. *CCH Congressional Index, Congressional Calendars, Digest of Public General*

Bills, Congressional Monitor, Congressional Information Service/Index, and *Congressional Record*).

(2) *U.S.C.C.A.N.*: Table of Enacted Bills.

(3) *Statutes at Large*: List of Bills Enacted into Public Law (beginning with 88th Congress, 1st Sess., 1963).

(b) **Public law number to bill number:**

(1) Slip laws and *Statutes at Large* at the head of the text.

(2) Public Law Table of *Digest of Public General Bills*.

(3) *Daily Digest* of *Congressional Record*: History of Bills Enacted into Public Law (see Exhibit 34 below).

(4) *U.S.C.C.A.N.*: Table of Public Laws.

(5) *C.C.H. Congressional Index*: Table of Enactments.

(6) *Congressional Information Service/Index.*

(c) **Bill number or public law number to Statutes at Large:**

(1) Text of Slip Law (since 1951).

(2) *Statutes at Large:* List of Public Laws.

(3) *U.S.C.C.A.N.:* Slip Law and Table of Public Laws.

(4) *U. S. Code:* Statutes included table, *Statutes at Large* (see Exhibit 20 above).

(d) **Bill number or public law number to Code:**
   (1) *U.S.C.C.A.N.:* Table of Classifications.
   (2) *U. S. Code:* Statutes Included Table. (First, Public Law number must be translated into *Statutes at Large* citation and then to the Code citation; see Exhibit 20).

(e) To go from *U. S. Code* sections to *Statutes at Large* citations—use parenthetical references following text of Code section.

3. Methods of Access to Statutory Material. Judicial decisions, as noted previously, can be located by their case name, by the legal concept involved, or by descriptive factual catchwords. Statutes can be approached in the same three ways, that is (a) by a citation table or popular name table; (b) through the relevant legal concept, by selecting the apparently pertinent title of the Code and using its analytical breakdowns to find the appropriate section; or (c) using the statutory word indexes to get directly to the relevant sections. The circuitous approach (b) suffers from the same disadvantage as approaching a case digest by its broad legal divisions rather than through the descriptive word index. It is almost always faster to use method (c) based on indexes which provide quick reference to relevant sections by specific catchwords and phrases.

4. Supplementation and Updating of Statutes. As we have noted, laws are being passed by Congress every year and by the various state legislatures in annual or biennial sessions. Hence there is need for constant supplementation to be sure that the statutory texts reflect the latest changes. A compilation of statutes which does not have internal supplementation is almost useless, unless it can be easily updated by some other means. Statutory supplementation is ordinarily provided by pocket parts inserted annually in the back of each volume; by pamphlets, such as the quarterly supplements to the *U.S.C.A.*; or by looseleaf, as in those few states which issue their statutes in that form (e. g. Alaska and Oregon). Statutes of some of the states are also updated by *session law services* which provide advance sheet pamphlets while the legislature is in session.

Shepard's state citators enable the researcher to determine whether there have been any changes in a statutory text, thereby updating the statute, but, of course, not providing the actual text of any changes recorded therein.

5. State Statutory Finding Tools. Research in state statutes involves very much the same techniques as in federal statutes, although the indexes, tables and other research aids are frequently less sophisticated in state materials.

State statutes can be searched in the following ways:

(a) By subject—via the general index of the various annotated codes and by the annual indexes in the session law volumes;

(b) By retrospective, cumulative statutory indexes which have been published from time to time in a few of the states;

(c) By indexes to the laws of more than one state (e. g. with the *State Law Index* during the period 1925 to 1948, and since 1963, with the *Computerized Law Index* and its predecessors;

(d) By popular name tables which are provided by *Shepard's Citations* and in the annotated codes of some states.

Cross references for state statutes, similar to those for federal, are provided in the following ways:

(a) **From session law citation to that of the code:** in the tables of the annotated codes.

(b) **From code to session law:** usually following the text of the code section in a footnote or parenthetical reference.

(c) **From an earlier code edition to a later revision or vice-versa:** by parallel conversion tables in the tables volume or individual title volumes of the annotated codes.

CITATORS FOR STATUTORY MATERIALS

Shepard's publishes statutory citators which perform much the same function as their case citators, although the former are somewhat more difficult to use because of the different statutory forms. There is a statutory citator for every state and for federal laws with the usual advance sheet supplementation to keep them up to date.

On the federal level, *Shepard's United States Citations* includes entries for every

CITATORS FOR STAT. MATERIALS Ch. 4

section of the *U. S. Code* and for every provision in the *Statutes at Large* which has not
been incorporated into the Code. Exhibits
27 and 28 show and explain those two types
of coverage.

UNITED STATES CODE
(Illustrative Statute)

United
States
Code, 1964
Edition
and
Supple-
ment, 1965

TITLE 42

§ 1975d

C363US420
C4LE1307
C80SC1502   2
C177FS817

46ABA39   4

Subsec. a   1
A78St251

318F2d656   3

Subsec. c   4
46ABA40

Subsec. d   5
5LE954n

Subsec. f
A78St252
C363US425
C4LE1312
C80SC1502
C177FS817
170FS64
Subsec. g
A78St252   7
C363US427
C4LE1313
C80SC1502
170FS64
176FS791
46ABA41
Subsec. i
Ad78St252

Citations to section "§" 1975d of Title 42 of the United
States Code, 1964 Edition and Supplement, 1965 are shown in
the left margin of this page in the same form in which they
appear in this volume. In Shepard's United States Citations,
Statute Edition any citation to a section of the United States
Code presently in effect is shown as is illustrated here and
any citation to a section of the United States Code no longer
in effect is shown as referring to the section number of the
United States Code of the year when that section number last
appeared.

Citations to each cited statutory provision are grouped
as follows:

1. amendments, repeals, etc. by acts of Congress subsequent to 1962;

2. citations by the United States Supreme Court and the
   lower federal courts analyzed as to constitutionality
   or validity;

3. other citations by the United States Supreme Court
   and the lower federal courts;

4. citations in articles in the American Bar Association
   Journal;

5. citations in annotations of the Lawyers' Edition,
   United States Supreme Court Reports and of the
   American Law Reports;

6. other citations in acts of Congress subsequent to 1962;
   and

7. citations to specific subdivisions.

For the purpose of illustration only, this grouping has been
indicated by bracketing the citations accordingly. It will be
noted that as yet there are no citations in group six.

Exhibit 27: *Shepard's* illustrative citator for the *U. S.
Code.*

[*109*]

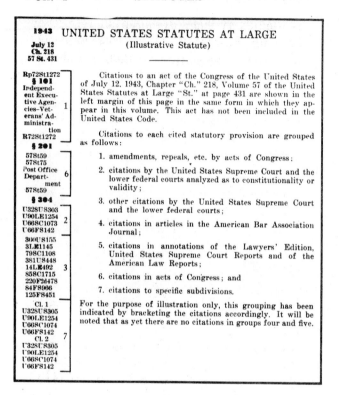

1943   UNITED STATES STATUTES AT LARGE
July 12   (Illustrative Statute)
Ch. 218
57 St. 431

Rp72St1272   Citations to an act of the Congress of the United States
§ 101   of July 12, 1943, Chapter "Ch." 218, Volume 57 of the United
Independ-   States Statutes at Large "St." at page 431 are shown in the
ent Execu-   left margin of this page in the same form in which they ap-
tive Agen-   1   pear in this volume. This act has not been included in the
cies–Vet-   United States Code.
erans' Ad-
ministra-
tion   Citations to each cited statutory provision are grouped
R72St1272   as follows:

§ 201

578t59   1. amendments, repeals, etc. by acts of Congress;
578t75
Post Office
Depart-   6   2. citations by the United States Supreme Court and the
ment   lower federal courts analyzed as to constitutionality or
578t59   validity;

§ 304

U32SUS303   3. other citations by the United States Supreme Court
U90LE1254   and the lower federal courts;
U66SC1073   2
U66FS142   4. citations in articles in the American Bar Association
    Journal;
300US155
31LE1145   5. citations in annotations of the Lawyers' Edition,
79SC1108   United States Supreme Court Reports and of the
381US448   American Law Reports;
14LE492   3
85SC1715   6. citations in acts of Congress; and
220F2d478
84FS966   7. citations to specific subdivisions.
125FS451

Cl. 1   For the purpose of illustration only, this grouping has been
U32SUS305   indicated by bracketing the citations accordingly. It will be
U90LE1254   noted that as yet there are no citations in groups four and five.
U66SC1074
U66FS142   7
Cl. 2
U32SUS305
U90LE1254
U66SC1074
U66FS142

Exhibit 28:   *Shepard's* illustrative citator for the
         U. S. Statutes at Large.

In the Shepard's state citators, statutes are usually listed by their citations in the latest form of subject compilation. Where the subject compilation is completely lacking in authority, as in Pennsylvania, they may use the session law approach. Even if the code is used as the basis of listing, there will still be many statutes not in the code which will be listed in Shepard's by their *session law* citation.

Shepard's Citations can be used and, in fact, often *must* be used for the following purposes: to verify the current status of particular laws; to trace the legislative and judicial history of particular laws to determine whether they have been changed by later enactments or interpretations; and to develop further research leads to judicial decisions, attorney general opinions or legal periodical articles.

Shepard's statutory citators cover the following classes of cited and citing materials:

CITED MATERIAL	CITING MATERIAL
Constitutions	Later statutes and legislative changes
Codes	
Session laws	Cases
Treaties	Legal periodicals
Administrative regulations	Opinions of the Attorney General
Local ordinances	
Court rules	
Patents	
Trade Marks	

Shepard's also uses the following symbols to indicate significant actions which have been taken with respect to a particular statute either by later legislative changes or court decisions:

ABBREVIATIONS—ANALYSIS
STATUTES

Form of Statute

Amend.	Amendment	¶	Paragraph	Subch.	Subchapter
Art.	Article	P. L.	Public Law	Subcl.	Subclause
Ch.	Chapter	Pr.L	Private Law	Subd.	Subdivision
Cl.	Clause	Proc.	Proclamation	Sub ¶	Subparagraph
Ex. Ord.	Executive Order	Pt.	Part	Subsec.	Subsection
H.C.R.	House Concur-	Res.	Resolution	Vet.Reg.	Veterans'
	rent Resolution	§	Section		Regulations
No.	Number	St.	Statutes at Large		

Operation of Statute
Legislative

A	(amended)	Statute amended.
Ad	(added)	New section added.
E	(extended)	Provisions of an existing statute extended in their application to a later statute or allowance of additional time for performance of duties required by a statute within a limited time.
L	(limited)	Provisions of an existing statute declared not to be extended in their application to a later statute.
PA	(proposed amendment)	Future action necessary to confirm or reject amendment.
PR	(proposed repeal)	Future action necessary to confirm or reject repeal.
R	(repealed)	Abrogation of an existing statute.
Re-en	(re-enacted)	Statute re-enacted.
Rn	(renumbered)	Renumbering of existing sections.
Rp	(repealed in part)	Abrogation of part of an existing statute.
Rs	(repealed and superseded)	Abrogation of an existing statute and substitution of new legislation therefor.
Rv	(revised)	Statute revised.
S	(superseded)	Substitution of new legislation for an existing statute not expressly abrogated.
Sd	(suspended)	Statute suspended.
Sdp	(suspended in part)	Statute suspended in part.
Sg	(supplementing)	New matter added to an existing statute.
Sp	(superseded in part)	Substitution of new legislation for part of an existing statute not expressly abrogated.

Judicial

C	Constitutional.	V Void or invalid.
U	Unconstitutional.	Va Valid.
Up	Unconstitutional in part.	Vp Void or invalid in part.

Exhibit 29: *Shepard's* Statutory Symbols with Notes.

Although Shepard's is the primary and indispensable citator in American legal research, there are other citators which may be useful for limited purposes. Looseleaf services frequently provide a citator of sorts for statutes in their fields. Because of the prompt supplementation of these services, they often inform the subscribers of changes in particular laws more quickly than that information is conveyed by Shepard's. In addition, the looseleaf services provide the text of the statute itself which can not be found in Shepard's. However, looseleaf services exist for only some subjects and even in those areas do not offer as complete coverage of citations to cases and other materials as does Shepard's.

For local ordinances, Shepard's introduced another service in 1969, *Ordinance Law Annotations*, which digests leading American state decisions that interpret or apply city and county ordinances. These annotations are arranged alphabetically by subject and provide a unique research tool which is closer to a digest than to the usual Shepard's citator. It is kept up to date by annual pocket parts.

CHAPTER V

LEGISLATIVE HISTORY

Statutory research often involves the investigation of the pre-enactment history of an existing statute or the current status of a proposed law which is then under consideration in the legislature. Both of these inquiries require the study of what we call "legislative history". The ambiguities which occur so frequently in the language of our laws also require lawyers and scholars to locate legislative documents from which they can learn the intent of Congress or a state legislature. There are thus two main purposes in this area of research: (a) to ascertain the status of a pending *bill* during the legislative session, or to follow the steps in its legislative progress; and (b) to determine the meaning or intent of a particular *enactment* from the documents of its consideration by the legislature.

SOURCES OF LEGISLATIVE HISTORY

The principal sources in which evidence of congressional intent may be sought are the following:

1. Presidential Messages. Although not legislative in origin, these documents accompany legislation proposed to Congress by the executive and often explain the purpose and intent of the draftsmen. They are printed and indexed in the *Congressional Record*, appear in the *Weekly Compilation of Presidential Documents*, and the *House* and *Senate Journals*, and are also issued as *House* and *Senate Documents*. Important messages are reproduced in the advance sheets of the *U. S. Code Congressional and Administrative News*. While only indirect evidence of congressional intent, they provide helpful background information for that purpose. Messages are also frequently issued when the President signs or vetoes enactments.

2. Congressional Bills. Differences between the several bills leading to a particular enactment may aid in determining legislative intent, since deletions, additions, or other variations in the bill at different stages of the legislative process imply deliberate choices of language by the legislators. The bills of each House are individually numbered in series and retain their identifying number and status through both sessions of a Congress. (The term of a Congress is two years, consisting of two one-year sessions.) Bills are received in the larger research law libraries in a slip form and can also be obtained individually from the clerk of the House or Senate, their sponsor, or the appropriate congressional committee, if requested promptly after their introduction. Commerce Clearing House through its costly *Legislative Reporting Service* also regularly supplies subscribers with bills on particular subjects. The form of a bill is shown in Exhibit 30 below:

Calendar No. 158

88TH CONGRESS
1ST SESSION

S. 1409

[Report No. 176]

IN THE SENATE OF THE UNITED STATES

APRIL 30, 1963

Mr. McNAMARA (for himself, Mr. MORSE, and Mr. RANDOLPH) introduced the following bill; which was read twice and referred to the Committee on Labor and Public Welfare

MAY 13, 1963

Reported by Mr. McNAMARA, with amendments

[Omit the part struck through and insert the part printed in italic]

A BILL

To prohibit discrimination on account of sex in the payment of wages by employers engaged in commerce or in the production of goods for commerce and to provide for the restitution of wages lost by employees by reason of any such discrimination.

1   *Be it enacted by the Senate and House of Representa-*

2   *tives of the United States of America in Congress assembled,*

3   That this Act may be cited as the "Equal Pay Act of 1963".

4   DECLARATION OF PURPOSE

5   SEC. 2. (a) The Congress hereby finds that the exist-

Exhibit 30: *A Congressional Bill.*

The bill number is used in all status tables and on most legislative documents to identify the proposed legislation. It also appears on the law after enactment, both in its slip form and in the bound volumes of the *Statutes at Large*.

3. Hearings. These are transcripts of testimony before Senate and House committees on proposed legislation or on a particular subject under congressional investigation. In addition to such testimony, exhibits contributed by interested individuals or groups are also included (e. g. letters, statements, statistical material, newspaper articles, etc.). The purpose of a hearing is to determine the need for new legislation or to bring before Congress information relevant to its preparation and enactment. Hearings are not, however, held for all legislation, nor are all hearings published.

A search for relevant hearings should not be limited to the session in which the particular law is enacted, since they may have extended over more than one session and been issued in multiple parts and volumes. There is no uniformity in the numbering of the various series of hearings issued by the committees of Congress, but they are generally identified by the *name of the committee* holding them, the *session* and *Congress* during which they are held, the *title* which appears on the cover, the *bill* on which they are being held, and the *date span* of the testimony.

Hearings are available from the committee conducting them; from the Government Printing Office; or occasionally from members of the committee. They are listed in the *Monthly Catalog of U. S. Government Publications* and since 1970 in the *Congressional Information Service/Index* by committee and are indexed there by subject. Exhibit 31 on page 120 shows the title page of a typical hearing:

EQUAL PAY ACT

HEARINGS

BEFORE THE

SPECIAL SUBCOMMITTEE ON LABOR

OF THE

COMMITTEE ON EDUCATION AND LABOR

HOUSE OF REPRESENTATIVES

EIGHTY-EIGHTH CONGRESS

FIRST SESSION

ON

H.R. 3861 and Related Bills

TO PROHIBIT DISCRIMINATION, ON ACCOUNT OF SEX,
IN THE PAYMENT OF WAGES BY EMPLOYERS ENGAGED
IN COMMERCE OR IN THE PRODUCTION OF GOODS FOR
COMMERCE AND TO PROVIDE FOR THE RESTITUTION OF
WAGES LOST BY EMPLOYEES BY REASON OF ANY SUCH
DISCRIMINATION

HEARINGS HELD IN WASHINGTON, D.C.,
MARCH 15, 25, 26, AND 27, 1963

Printed for the use of the Committee on Education and Labor

ADAM C. POWELL, *Chairman*

U.S. GOVERNMENT PRINTING OFFICE
WASHINGTON : 1963

97269

Exhibit 31: Title page of a Hearing.

The *Monthly Catalog*, incidentally, is the most complete listing of all U. S. Government documents and includes many documents of legal significance. It is issued monthly with a detailed subject and author index and its December issue contains a cumulative index of the entire year. It is a particularly important finding tool for legislative material, since it lists each individual committee report, document, published hearing, message and enactment, as they are published. There is often, however, a substantial time lag between publication and listing, during which the supply of documents may be exhausted. The *Catalog* also includes some publications which are not on sale or publicly available, although its statements as to availability and source are not always accurate.

4. Committee Reports. These are issued by the congressional committees of both houses (and by conference committees of the two houses) on each bill reported out of committee for action. Reports frequently include the text of the bill, describe its contents and purposes, and give reasons for the committee's recommendations (sometimes including a *Minority View*). They are also issued by committees on various investigations, studies and hearings not related to a particular bill under consideration. Committee reports are published in a numbered series and are listed in the *Monthly Catalog* and the *Congressional Information Service/Index*.

Reports are sometimes available from the committee issuing them or from the clerk of the House or Senate, as the case may be. Many are placed on sale and can be purchased from the Government Printing Office. Reports on the most important enactments are also published selectively in the *U. S. Code Congressional and Administrative News* and all appear subsequently in the bound official *Serial Set,* along with *House* and *Senate Documents*. They are usually identified by House, Congress, session and report number, e. g. House Report No. 309, 88th Congress, 1st Session. A typical report is illustrated in Exhibit 32 below.

5. Debates. The *Congressional Record* is a verbatim transcript of legislative debates and proceedings, subject to revision by the members of Congress. It is published each day that one or both houses are in session. In addition, the appendix to the *Congressional Record* includes extensions of floor remarks, exhibits from legislators, communications on pending legislation and almost any other material a congressman wishes to get into the Record. There is a *Daily Digest* in each issue, a fortnightly index, and at the end

| 88TH CONGRESS | HOUSE OF REPRESENTATIVES | REPORT |
| 1st Session | | No. 309 |

EQUAL PAY ACT OF 1963

MAY 20, 1963.—Committed to the Committee of the Whole House on the State of the Union and ordered to be printed

Mr. POWELL, from the Committee on Education and Labor, submitted the following

REPORT

[To accompany H.R. 6060]

The Committee on Education and Labor, to whom was referred the bill (H.R. 6060) to prohibit discrimination on account of sex in the payment of wages by employers engaged in commerce or in the production of goods for commerce, having considered the same, report favorably thereon without amendment and recommend that the bill do pass.

BACKGROUND

Legislation to eliminate wage discrimination based upon sex of the employee has been recommended by the present and two immediately preceding administrations.

During World War II the War Labor Board promulgated and administered an "equal pay for women" policy.

During the 87th Congress the Committee on Education and Labor considered a number of "equal pay" bills, reported favorably to the House of Representatives and a bill was enacted. The other body also acted favorably on "equal pay" legislation, but its affirmative action took the form of an amendment to a House-approved bill, the subject matter of which was outside the jurisdiction of the Committee on Education and Labor.

Exhibit 32: A Congressional Report.

of the session, a bound edition made up of over 30 volumes which include a cumulative index (with entries by subject, title and congressman), a cumulation of the Daily Digest, and a complete History of Bills and Resolutions for that session. The appendix is no longer included in the bound set, although the Index still cites to it. It is available on microfilm, however.

The *Congressional Record* differs from the *House* and *Senate Journals* in that the journals do not include the verbatim debates. The journals merely record the proceedings, indicate whether there was debate, and report the resulting action and votes taken. The *Congressional Record* never contains hearings and only on rare occasions reports. Some bills are read into the *Record*, but it is not to be considered a major source for bills. Its importance is primarily as a report of debates and actions taken.

The predecessors of the *Congressional Record*, which began in 1873, are: the *Annals of Congress* (1789–1824); the *Register of Debates* (1824–1873); and the *Congressional Globe* (1833–1873).

6. House and Senate Documents. The document series include reports of some congressional investigations not in the regular committee reports. They also contain presidential messages, special studies or exhibits prepared by or at the request of Congress, and communications from executive departments or agencies. They are listed in the

Monthly Catalog and in the *Congressional Information Service/Index*, and are published by the Government Printing Office in a numbered series for each house and Congress. Identification is by house, Congress, session, and document number, similar to the Report series.

7. Senate Executive Documents and Reports. These are restricted or confidential publications of the Senate forming an essential part of the legislative histories of treaties. The Executive Documents contain the treaties and related correspondence from the President and Secretary of State. The reports are issued by the Foreign Relations Committee on individual treaties. Only when released by the Senate are they listed in the *Monthly Catalog* and made available to the public. The Senate Executive Reports are numbered, while the Documents receive an alphabetical designation. Both also require the Congress and session number for identification.

OUTLINE OF LEGISLATIVE STEPS AND RELEVANT DOCUMENTS

An understanding of the legislative process is essential for one working in this field. Each of the relevant documents of legislative history can be associated with the stage of law-making at which it is issued. The following are the most significant steps and their related documents:

Action	Document
Preliminary Inquiry	Hearings on the general subject of the proposed legislation. (N. B. Relevant hearings may have been held in a previous Congressional session or may run through several sessions.)
Executive Recommendation	Presidential Message proposing an administration bill.
Introduction of Bill	Original text—Slip Bill as introduced.
Referred to Committee	Committee Print of Bill.
Hearings on Bill	Hearings — published transcript and exhibits, sometimes including a Hearing Print of Bill.
Executive Agency Recommendations	House or Senate Document or in Congressional Record Appendix.
Reported out of Committee	Committee Report including Committee's version or Reported Print of Bill.
Legislative Debates	*Congressional Record*, sometimes including texts of bill in amended forms.
Passage or defeat	Final House or Senate version of bill.
Other House	Generally same procedure and documents as above.
Referred to Conference Committee (if texts passed by each House differ)	Conference Committee version of bill; Conference Committee Report.

Action	Document
Passage by 2nd House	Enrolled Bill signed by Speaker of House or President of Senate and then sent to President (not available to public).
If vetoed	Presidential Veto Message.
If approved by President	Slip law (also *USCCAN* & *FCA* advance sheet). Subsequently bound into *Statutes at Large* and annual volumes of *USCCAN* and *FCA*. Then classified in the appropriate titles of the *U. S. Code* and its unofficial, annotated editions. Presidential Message may also be issued on signing of the law.

STATUS TABLES

The essential finding tools for locating and tracing congressional bills and their legislative history are status tables, which are published in a variety of forms. Status tables are lists of pending bills and resolutions, with statements of the actions taken thereon and references to the documents which reflect such actions. They are arranged by bill numbers and often include a short digest of each bill. Status tables enable the researcher to trace the history of a bill or locate legislative documents which may aid in ascertaining its congressional intent. The following are the most useful of these tables:

1. Congressional Record—History of Bills and Resolutions. This table is published

fortnightly in the Index to the *Record* and
then cumulated for each session in the bound
Index volume. It lists actions taken on all
pending bills and resolutions, including page
references to the *Record*, dates, and report
numbers. The final cumulative *History* for
each session is very useful for retrospective
histories and is weak only in lacking references to hearings. The fortnightly listings
are less helpful, because they do not cumulate. This table is illustrated in Exhibit 33
below:

SENATE BILLS

S. 1406—Continued
   Mr. Bible; Committee on the District of Columbia, 7293.—Reported with amendments (S. Rept. 656), 22665.—Amended and passed Senate, 22794.—Referred to House Committee on the District of Columbia, 22962.

'S. 1407—For the relief of Rafael I. Fernandez.
   Mr. Smathers; Committee on the Judiciary, 7293.—Reported (S. Rept. 223), 10247.—Passed Senate, 10599.—Referred to House Committee on the Judiciary, 10740.

S. 1408—To amend section 312 of title 38, United States Code, to provide that leukemia developing a 10-percent degree of disability after separation from the service shall be considered to be service connected.

   Mr. Smathers: Committee on Finance, 7293.

S. 1409—To prohibit discrimination on account of sex in the payment of wages by employers engaged in commerce or in the production of goods for commerce and to provide for the restitution of wages lost by employees by reason of any such discrimination.

   Mr. McNamara, Mr. Morse, and Mr. Randolph; Committee on Labor and Public Welfare, 7293.—Reported with amendment (S. Rept. 176), 8264.—Debated, 8866, 8892, 8913.—Amended and passed Senate 8916.—Amended and passed House (in lieu of H.R. 6060), 9217.—Title amended, 9218.—Senate concurs in House amendment, 9761.—Examined and signed, 9854, 9941.—Presented to the President, 9970.—Approved [Public Law 88–38], 10440.

Exhibit 33: *History of Bills and Resolutions* table in the *Congressional Record*.

2. Congressional Record—Daily Digest.

These daily summaries of congressional activity are published in each issue of the *Record* and include a subject index which serves as a status table for bills *acted upon*. The *Daily Digest* cumulates at the end of each session into a separate bound volume of the *Record* which contains the final *History of Bills Enacted into Public Law*.   This table is a useful one, although it lacks the debate references found in the *History of Bills and Resolutions*.   It is illustrated in Exhibit 34 *below*.

3.   Digest of Public General Bills.   This publication of the Library of Congress is primarily useful for its synopses of public bills and resolutions, with somewhat fuller digests of reported measures.   The Digest also includes a status table of all public bills upon which action has been taken.   Issued only 8–10 times a year, it is less useful than those tools which are issued more frequently. However, a final issue cumulates the digests and tables and is helpful for retrospective searches.

4.   Legislative Calendars (For the House, Senate and various committees).   Each House and most committees issue calendars of pending business.   These contain very useful status tables, including the House of Representatives *Numerical Order of Bills and Resolutions Which Have Passed Either or Both Houses, and Bills Now Pending on the Calendar*.   This status table is particularly valuable because of its frequency.   It appears daily, is cumulative, and includes reported

[*130*]

HISTORY OF BILLS ENACTED INTO PUBLIC LAW (88TH CONG., 1ST SESS.)—Continued

Title	Bill No.	Date introduced	Committee hearings		Date reported		Report No.		Page of Congressional Record of passage		Date of passage		Public Law	
			House	Senate	House	Senate	House	Senate	House	Senate	House	Senate	Date approved	No.
Authorizing funds for procurement of aircraft, missiles, and naval vessels for fiscal year 1964.	H.R. 2440	Jan. 21	AS	AS	Mar. 6	Apr. 9	61	113	4091	6432	Mar. 13	Apr. 11	May 23	88-28
To provide for the development of Federal and State outdoor recreation programs.	S. 20 (H.R. 1762)	Jan. 14	IIA	IIA	Mar. 28	Feb. 28	160	11	7246	3899	Apr. 29	Mar. 11	May 28	88-29
Providing a temporary increase in the public debt limit.	H.R. 6009	May 2	WM	Fin	May 6	May 23	277	186	8560	9740	May 15	May 28	May 29	88-30
Reduction of temporary additional Federal unemployment tax and authorization of employment security administrative expenses.	H.R. 4655	Mar. 7	WM	Fin	Apr. 11	May 9	211	174	7219	9459	Apr. 29	May 14	May 29	88-31
Providing a 3-year suspension of duty on corkboard insulation and cork stoppers.	H.R. 2053	Jan. 17	WM	Fin	Feb. 4	Apr. 15	26	160	2022	7188	Feb. 26	Apr. 16	May 29	88-32
To change the name of Harpers Ferry National Monument to Harpers Ferry National Historical Park.	S. 18	Jan. 14	IIA	IIA	May 13	Apr. 8	291	114	8912	6006	May 20	Apr. 9	May 29	88-33
Authorizing a survey and establishment of a townsite for the Juneau Indian Village, Alaska.	S. 247	Jan. 15	IIA	IIA	May 14	Apr. 8	294	124	8933	6454	May 20	Apr. 11	May 29	88-34
Authorizing the sale of certain public lands in Nevada to Lincoln County.	S. 873 (H.R. 4131)	Feb. 20	IIA	IIA	Apr. 29	Apr. 9	251	119	7811	6432	May 6	Apr. 11	May 29	88-35
To repeal the silver purchase acts and the related transfer tax on silver bullion.	H.R. 5389	Apr. 2	BC	BC	Apr. 3	May 13	183	175	6167	9372	Apr. 10	May 23	June 4	88-36
To consolidate the Vicksburg National Military Park and provide for adjustments necessitated by the installation of a park tour road.	S. 386 (H.R. 1162)	Jan. 21	IIA	IIA	May 13	Apr. 8	292	115	8956	6540	May 20	Apr. 10	June 4	88-37
To prohibit discrimination based on sex in wages paid for employment in interstate commerce.	S. 1409 (H.R. 6060)	Apr. 30	E&L	L&PW	May 20	May 13	309	176	9217	8916	May 23	May 17	June 10	88-38
Fiscal 1964 appropriations for the Department of the Treasury and Post Office, the Executive Office of the President, and certain independent agencies.	H.R. 5366	Apr. 1	App	App	Apr. 1	May 1	179	168	5772	8030	Apr. 4	May 8	June 13	88-39
To extend grants-in-aid to the Republic of the Philippines for hospitalization of Commonwealth Army veterans.	H.R. 240 (S. 331)	Jan. 9	VA	L&PW	Mar. 6	May 27	70	190	5186	10047	Apr. 1	June 4	June 13	88-40
Authorizing the lending of certain military equipment to the	H.R. 2439	Jan. 21	AS	AS	Jan. 29	June 4	4	206	1632	10592	Feb. 4	June 11	June 21	88-41

Exhibit 34: *Daily Digest: History of Bills Enacted into Public Law.*

bills of both the House and Senate. The final issue comes out *before* the bound volumes of the *Congressional Record* and includes actions during both sessions of Congress. It does not include all bills introduced, but only those on which action was taken. Committee calendars are usually the best source of information on hearings.

5. Congressional Information Service/Index. This looseleaf service, begun in 1970, offers detailed indexing of congressional hearings, reports and documents, as well as status tables of pending *active* bills. The service is supplemented monthly, with quarterly and annual cumulations. The annual volumes include an excellent summary of legislative history of enacted laws, with hearing references. Both the monthly issues and the annual cumulation provide the best available summary of all hearings held, arranged by bill number.

6. CCH Congressional Index (Commerce Clearing House, Inc.). This commercial service is a very popular index to current legislative history. It does not, however, contain the actual texts of either bills, debates or reports. Its looseleaf format permits convenient weekly supplementation of all of its indexes and tables in two volumes. It includes an index of public general bills, a status table of actions taken thereon, an index of enactments, a table of companion bills, a list of pending treaties, voting records, and other useful legislative information. It also contains hearing references which appear in few other status tables. Separate volumes are issued for each Congress.

Number 87—73 2-12-64	Legislative History of Senate Bills	3705

To H. Agriculture 7/15/63
Reptd., with amend., H. Rept. 597 .. 7/29/63
Passed H., as reptd. [Voice].......... 8/5/63
H. amend., agreed to by S. 8/8/63
Approved [Public Law 88-99] 8/19/63

1409
Reptd., with amend., S. Rept. 176 .. 5/13/63
Passed S., as reptd. [Voice] 5/17/63
Amended on H. Floor [Voice] 5/23/63
Passed H., with amend., in lieu of H. R. 6060 [Voice] 5/23/63
H. amend. agreed to by S. 5/28/63
To President 5/29/63
Approved [Public Law 88-38] 6/10/63

1523
Reptd., with amend., S. Rept. 271 .. 6/19/63

H. hearing available 9/9/63
Reptd., no amend., H. Rept. 629 ..... 8/1/63
Passed H., without amend. [Roll-call]
.... 8/5/63
Approved [Public Law 88-100] 8/19/63

1698
Hearing in S. 9/23/63
S. hearing available 11/8/63
Reptd., no amend., S. Rept. 663 ... 11/26/63
Passed S., without amend. [Voice] .....
.... 12/3/63
To H. Merchant Marine and Fisheries
.... 12/4/63
Reptd., no amend., H. Rept. 1028 . 12/12/63
Passed H., without amend. [Voice] ......
.... 12/17/63
To President 12/19/63

Exhibit 35: *CCH Congressional Index*, Table of Senate Bills.

7. U. S. Code Congressional and Administrative News (West Publishing Company).

The great value of this service, as noted above, is its publication of the *texts* of enacted public laws and of selective congressional committee reports on the more important acts. None of the previously mentioned publications in this section includes the actual texts of the documents. The biweekly advance sheets of *U.S.C.C.A.N.* during the congressional session and its cumulative bound volumes at the end of the session include status tables and histories of enactments which are less useful than most of those described above, however.

8. Congressional Quarterly Weekly Report. This weekly commercial publication summarizes activities concerning important legislation. It contains a status table of major legislation, arranged by subject of the bill, which indicates House and Senate activity and current status. In the body of the publication are brief digests of legislation and news developments. There is cumulative indexing and a final *Almanac* which lists a variety of material of permanent value relating to the activities of Congress during the preceding year. It contains legislative histories, pertinent background material relating to legislation and an index to all public law.

9. Congressional Monitor. This *daily* congressional service covers all active legislation. It includes summaries of each day's scheduled activity in the committees, actions concluded on the previous day on the floor, forecasts of expected activity, excerpts of important congressional documents, a weekly list of printed hearings, reports and other legislative documents, and a weekly status table of active bills arranged by broad subject groupings. The status table does not cite to debates, but does include committee reports and hearing references.

INDEXES TO HEARINGS

Because most status tables do not include complete information about hearings held on a particular bill or on a subject related to future legislation, the researcher needs other approaches to this source of legislative history.

The monthly indexes and the annual cumulative index of the *Monthly Catalog of U. S. Government Publications* include references to hearings published during the periods covered. They are perhaps the best source for detailed information on published hearings, but do not, however, include listings by bill number.

Congressional Information Service (CIS Index) offers a new legislative approach which includes good indexing to congressional hearings by subject, bill number, committee and title.

The U. S. Senate Library publishes an extremely useful retrospective index to the hearings of both Houses entitled *Cumulative Index of Congressional Committee Hearings.* It is arranged in three parts—by subject, bill number and committee. This index was first published in 1935, covering hearings as far back as the 41st Congress. Its various supplements include hearings from 1935 to date —the latest Quadrennial Supplement having been issued in 1967.

COMPILED LEGISLATIVE HISTORIES

The legislative histories of a few important laws have been compiled and published in book form. These compilations may include some or all of the important bills, debates, committee reports, hearings, etc. Such collections save the researcher the considerable time and trouble of compiling relevant references and documents himself. Some are published by government agencies, e. g. the National Labor Relations Board's excellent 2-volume histories of the Wagner Act, the Taft-Hartley Act, and the Labor-Management Reporting and Disclosure Act of 1959. Others are issued commercially, e. g. Seidman's *Legislative History of Federal Income and Excess Profits Laws, 1953–1939* (Prentice-Hall, 1954) in 2 volumes.

The Law Librarian's Society of Washington, D. C. issues a *Union List of Legislative Histories* (3rd ed., 1968) which lists unpublished legislative histories available in its libraries. In addition, *Microcard Editions* publishes in microfacsimile the *Legislative Histories of Internal Revenue Acts* and another more general microcard series called *Legislative History Service*, which compiles histories of the important enactments of each congressional session since the 82nd Congress in 1951–2.

There is, unfortunately, no single checklist of all available compiled legislative histories. Before beginning an extensive legislative history project, a researcher should always consult a law librarian for information as to whether there is an already compiled history.

STATE LEGISLATIVE HISTORY

The search for legislative history on the state level is a very difficult and frequently impossible task. Although almost every state has a legislative journal, only a few of these actually include the transcript of the debates. Bills are usually available from the state legislatures on request, but are not widely distributed and hence hard to locate after enactment. Committee reports are published in only a few states and hearings even more rarely.

There are status tables or digests of current bills published in a number of states, either officially by the state or by a private publisher. Perhaps the best sources of legislative history are the session law services published in connection with some of the annotated statutory codes. West issues several of these, which are among the best. C.C.H. publishes loose-leaf services containing just the text of current enactments for many of the states.

Official agencies for the recommendation and drafting of new legislation have appeared in many states. These may be independent agencies (such as some of the law revision commissions); or be attached to the judiciary (such as judicial councils); or function as branches of the legislatures (like the legislative councils). Such groups recommend new rules or legislation and prepare drafts of bills designed to implement their proposals. Their studies are, of course, persuasive with the legislatures and their recommendations are often enacted into law. In such a case the published report of the commission or council may provide an invaluable source of legislative history of the resultant enactment.

Since the available materials and tools for research in legislative history vary widely from state to state, one should familiarize himself with the sources that exist in his state. Frequently the state law library or legislative reference library offer useful assistance in this area.

CHAPTER VI

ADMINISTRATIVE LAW

Although administrative and executive agencies have existed since the creation of our country, their real growth began with the Industrial Revolution in the late 19th century. At that time, the increasingly complex problems of society and economy led to an expansion of the traditional functions of executive departments and to the creation of many new administrative agencies. In the 20th century, two World Wars and an economic depression accelerated this development and brought about a tremendous proliferation of their documentary output, most of which is of legal significance.

The regulatory agencies were created by Congress to carry out new economic legislation when it became apparent that Congress and the courts lacked the flexibility, expertise, time and manpower to handle this task. To do their work, the agencies were given the power to promulgate regulations and, when it appeared that these had been violated, to hold quasi-judicial hearings. Their orders, regulations and decisions have the force of law and form an important segment of legal bibliography.

Administrative agencies exist on all levels of our political system: in the federal government, where their forms of publication are fairly good; in the states, where administrative regulations and decisions are often difficult to locate; and on the local level, where published texts of regulations and decisions are virtually non-existent.

EXECUTIVE DOCUMENTS

In addition to the independent agencies and executive departments, the President of the United States also functions as a law-maker in his own right. In that capacity, he issues a variety of legally significant documents, most of which since 1965 appear promptly in an official publication, the *Weekly Compilation of Presidential Documents,* available from the Government Printing Office. In addition, they also appear in the following other sources:

1. Executive Orders and Presidential Proclamations are found in the *Federal Register*, the *Code of Federal Regulations* and in other services; Proclamations also appear in the *Statutes at Large.*

2. Presidential Messages are found in the *Congressional Record, House and Senate Journals, House and Senate*

Documents and selectively in the advance sheets of the *U.S.C.C.A.N.*

3. Reorganization Plans are found in the *Statutes at Large, U.S.C.C.A.N., Federal Register, Code of Federal Regulations* (Title 3), and *U.S.C.* (Title 5).

4. Treaties and Executive Agreements, since 1950, are published in slip form and in a bound series, *U. S. Treaties and Other International Agreements*; before that date in the *Statutes at Large.*

In recent years an official series called *Public Papers of the Presidents* has also been published by the Government Printing Office. It contains collections of presidential documents, arranged by year, for presidents after Franklin D. Roosevelt. These volumes, which are individually indexed, contain most of the documents listed above. With the exception of the texts of Executive Orders and Proclamations, they cumulate the contents of the *Weekly Compilation of Presidential Documents.* So far, the papers of Presidents Truman, Eisenhower, Kennedy, Johnson and Nixon have been published and the project will continue to issue the state papers of future presidents. Those of most of the earlier presidents are generally available in private editions.

FEDERAL ADMINISTRATIVE REGULATIONS

1. Federal Register. As more and more executive and administrative orders and regulations were promulgated in the early New Deal period it became increasingly difficult to locate copies and to know which were in effect at any particular time. There was no requirement that regulations be centrally filed, nor that they be published either as issued or in a compiled form. Public indignation arose over the confusion, uncertainty, and inaccessibility of these legal sources. Two important cases reached the U. S. Supreme Court where it was discovered that the administrative regulations on which they were based no longer were in effect. Newspapers throughout the country and opponents of the government criticized it for prosecuting people under non-existent laws. This furor led in 1935 to the enactment of the Federal Register Act which established the *Federal Register* as a daily gazette for executive and administrative promulgations. Executive orders and administrative regulations must be published in the *Federal Register* if they are to be legally effective. A

1937 amendment to the Act created the *Code of Federal Regulations,* which arranged the effective regulations in an indexed subject compilation with provision for supplementation. The *Federal Register,* pursuant to its authorizing legislation contains the following documents:

- (a) Presidential proclamations and executive orders of general applicability and legal effect;

- (b) Such other documents as the President may determine from time to time have general applicability and legal effect;

- (c) Such documents as may be required to be published by act of Congress;

- (d) Other documents selected by the director of the *Federal Register.*

For the purpose of inclusion in the *Register* the following are considered to have general applicability and legal effect:

"Every document issued under proper authority prescribing a penalty or a course of conduct, conferring a right, privilege, authority, or immunity, or imposing an obligation, and relevant or applicable to the general public, the members of a class, or the persons of a locality, as distinguished

from named individuals or organizations
* * * " (1 C.F.R. 11.2).

The *Federal Register* has been published
continuously since March 14, 1936 and provides a chronological source, similar to a
session law text, for these documents. Indexing has improved over the years until now
each daily issue contains its own subject index as well as two Codification Guides noting
which regulations have been changed in that
issue and which changed since the beginning
of the month. In addition, at the end of each
month, a monthly index is published along
with a Codification Guide which cumulates
references to all changes since the first of
the year. The Codification Guides, which are
the basic finding tool for locating changes
in the *Register*, are based on the titles and
sections of the *Code of Federal Regulations*.

The text of material in the *Federal Register* is *prima facie* evidence of its filing. If
a regulation is not filed therein, it is not
binding unless one can be shown to have had
actual knowledge of the regulation. Because
of the great bulk of the *Register* and because
of the poor quality of paper used, more and
more libraries are purchasing a microcard
edition of the *Register* and keeping only the
annual index and List of CFR Sections Affected (Codification Guide) in its original
form as a finding tool for the microcards.

CUMULATIVE LIST OF CFR PARTS AFFECTED—MAY

The following numerical guide is a list of the parts of each title of the Code of Federal Regulations affected by documents published to date during May.

	Page		Page		Page
5 CFR		**14 CFR—Continued**		**32 CFR**	
213	6215	Proposed Rules:		163	6161
7 CFR		39	6188	**33 CFR**	
54	6207	67	6188	203	6161
55	6141, 6207	71	6189, 6325	207	6161
56	6207	**19 CFR**		**36 CFR**	
70	6207	10	6149	311	6161
81	6207	**21 CFR**		**47 CFR**	
210	6207	121	6215	2	6215
717	6144	**26 CFR**		Proposed Rules:	
724	6144, 6146, 6207	1	6216	2	6219
908	6148	Proposed Rules:	6217		6226
910	6148	250		**49 CFR**	
Proposed Rules:		1	6222	95	6220
1040	6163	31	6322	141	6162
1042	6163	301	6323	**50 CFR**	
12 CFR		**29 CFR**		60	6218
12	6160	604	6216	Proposed Rules:	6216
14 CFR		606		60	6149
39	6150	Proposed Rules:		32	6224
71	6150, 6215	657	6224		6225
75	6150	697	6225		
97	6151				

Exhibit 36: List of CFR Sections Affected (Codification Guide) for Current Month.

The *Federal Register* has a permanent reference value and consequently should be accessible in some form. Its value stems from the fact that it includes some material which never appears in its companion publication, the *Code of Federal Regulations,* and it provides the only complete history of the regulations with the text of all changes.

2. Code of Federal Regulations. In 1937, realizing the limitations of chronological publication and the need for a permanent subject compilation of current regulations, Congress established the *Code of Federal Regulations.* The first edition came out in 1938 and was supplemented for many years. In 1949 the present second edition was published and it has been kept up to date since then by a process of perpetual revision. It is divided into some 50 titles some of which duplicate the titles of the *U. S. Code.* Each title is divided into chapters, parts and sections and the citation form is to title and section, e. g. 12 C.F.R. 25.2. The set is completely revised each year by the issuance of new pamphlets. These contain the text of new and amended rules as they exist on January 1 of each new year.

They do not reflect all of the changes which may have been made during the year and which were then modified again. The *Federal Register* therefore remains the only source for obtaining *all* of the different versions which may have been in effect, even briefly, during the year.

There is a General Index volume to the *C.F.R.* which does not, unfortunately, provide the detailed analysis necessary for really specific access. As with life in general, perhaps we must be thankful for what we have and remember the difficult days before 1935 when things were much worse. Each volume contains a *List of Sections Affected,* which tells the researcher at a glance whether particular sections have been affected by changes in that volume. These lists are cumulated and published in a separate volume covering 1949 to 1963—*List of Sections Affected, 1949–1963* (Wash., G.P.O. 1966). From 1964 to date, the lists appear in each volume of the *C.F.R.*

There are also many tables in the Code which enable the researcher to convert or move from one legal form to another. The following parallel references can be obtained in this way:

   (a) **Statute to rule:** from *U.S.C.* title and section to the related *C.F.R.* title and section (in Title 2, *C.F.R.*).

   (b) **Statute to executive order or proclamation:** from the act by its date and *Statutes at Large* citation to related executive orders or proclamations by number (in the compilation volume of Title 3, *C.F.R.*).

(c) **Proclamation, executive order or reorganization plan:** to their text in the *C.F.R.* (in Title 3, *C.F.R.*).

(d) **Proclamation, order or plan:** to their text or authorization in the *U. S. Code* (in the tables volumes of the *U.S.C.* and *U.S.C.A.*).

(e) **C.F.R. sections to their statutory or presidential authority:** (by note before each *C.F.R.* part, or after each *C.F.R.* section, under "Authority").

(f) **C.F.R. sections to their Federal Register source:** (by note before *C.F.R.* part or after *C.F.R.* section, under "Source").

The format of the *C.F.R.* can be seen in Exhibit 37 which follows:

PART 6—TRAFFIC IN CONTRABAND ARTICLES IN FEDERAL PENAL AND CORRECTIONAL INSTITUTIONS

§ 6.1   Consent of warden or superintendent required.

The introduction or attempt to introduce into or upon the grounds of any Federal penal or correctional institution or to take or attempt to take or send therefrom anything whatsoever without the knowledge and consent of the warden or superintendent of such Federal penal or correctional institution is prohibited. (Pub. Law 772, 80th Cong.; 18 U.S.C. 1791)

[13 F.R. 5660, Sept. 30, 1948]

CROSS REFERENCE: For Organization Statement, Bureau of Prisons, see Subpart Q of Part 0 of this Chapter.

PART 7—REWARDS FOR CAPTURE OF ESCAPED FEDERAL PRISONERS

Sec.
7.1   Standing offer of reward.
7.2   Amount of reward.
7.3   Eligibility for reward.
7.4   Procedure for claiming reward.
7.5   Certification.

AUTHORITY: The provisions of this Part 7 issued under sec. 161, R.S.; 18 U.S.C. 3059.

SOURCE: The provisions of this Part 7 appear at 25 F.R. 2420, Mar. 23, 1960.

CROSS REFERENCE: For Organization Statement, Bureau of Prisons, see Subpart Q of Part 0 of this Chapter.

intimidation, terrorizing, risks, etc., will be considered in determining the appropriate amount of reward.

§ 7.3   Eligibility for reward.

A reward may be paid to any person, except an official or employee of the Department of Justice or a law-enforcement officer of the United States Government, who personally captures and surrenders an escaped Federal prisoner to proper officials, or who assists in the capture, of an escaped Federal prisoner.

§ 7.4   Procedure for claiming reward.

A person claiming a reward under this part shall present his claim, within six months from the date of the capture, in the form of a letter to the Warden or United States Marshal concerned. The letter shall state fully the facts and circumstances on which the claim is based, and shall include the name of each escapee captured and the time and place of the capture, and details as to how the arrest was made by the claimant or as to how assistance was rendered to others who made the arrest.

§ 7.5   Certification.

The claim letter required under § 7.4 shall contain the following certification immediately preceding the signature of the claimant:

I am not an officer or employee of the Department of Justice or a law-enforcement officer of the United States Government.

Exhibit 37: A page in the *Code of Federal Regulations.*

Since title numbers and section numbers of the *Code of Federal Regulations* are used in the Codification Guides of the *Federal Register* as a means of identifying subsequent changes in those sections, the *F.R.* is really a daily supplement to the *C.F.R.* Without the Code, however, it would be virtually impossible to research federal regulations, since only it provides the current text with subject access.

In order to make a complete search for a current regulation, the researcher follows these steps:

(a) Consult the General Index volume of the *C.F.R.* to ascertain the relevant title.

(b) Check the *List of Sections Affected* in the latest revision to see whether the sections have been modified. If affected, examine the text of the section in that volume.

(c) Use the Codification Guide of the *Federal Register* at the end of the last preceding month to supplement the latest *C.F.R.* volume for any changes between January 1st and the end of the last month.

(d) Check the Codification Guide of the last daily issue of the *Register* to obtain changes since the first of the present month.

3. Looseleaf Publication of Regulations. Administrative regulations also appear in the commercially published looseleaf services which are dealt with in the next chapter. In that form, the regulations are well indexed and supplemented frequently, usually weekly.

For those reasons and also because of their integration with other relevant source material, regulations are widely used in that form. Unfortunately, the looseleaf services are not available for every subject field and are quite expensive.

4. Agency Publication of Regulations. The agencies themselves often publish texts of their regulations—in either looseleaf or pamphlet form. However, these publications are not well supplemented and, although relatively inexpensive, are not widely used by lawyers or legal scholars.

GOVERNMENT ORGANIZATION MANUAL

The *Government Organization Manual* is an annual directory of general information about the federal government, with primary emphasis upon the executive branch and regulatory agencies. (It also contains some information about Congress and the judiciary.) Each executive department and agency is described fully with the following coverage:

1. Citations to relevant statutes creating and affecting the agency.

2. Descriptions of the functions and authority of the agency.

3. Information about subsidiary units, bureaus, and predecessor agencies.

4. Names and functions of major officials.

5. Organizational charts.

6. Bibliographies of major publications.

The *Government Organization Manual* is one of the most important reference books of the federal government and is the third major publication of the Federal Register System. It can often save a researcher considerable time by providing quick answers to questions which might otherwise require extensive research.

ADMINISTRATIVE DECISIONS AND RULINGS

In addition to their legislative output, administrative agencies also issue decisions and rulings in the course of their quasi-judicial functions.

Most federal agencies now publish an official edition of those decisions in a form similar to that of the official state reports of court decisions. These reports are in chronological series, usually published first in an advance sheet or slip decision form and then in bound volumes. They are cited like court decisions, but with only the name of the private party involved in the proceeding, e. g. General Electric Co., 18 F.T.C. 501 (1958). The bound volumes usually contain subject indexes, but these do not cumulate. Adequate cumulative digests providing subject access to these chronologically published decisions are rare, although one or two agencies (e. g. the N.L.R.B.) do issue their own digests periodically. Subject access to the decisions of most agencies is effectively provided only by the privately published looseleaf services.

There are unofficial publications of some administrative decisions in the following forms:

1. Many looseleaf services publish decisions of administrative agencies in their subject fields (e. g. *CCH Trade Regulation Service* which publishes decisions of the Federal Trade Commission). These usually contain better indexing than the official edition, appear more promptly, and contain other useful research material (e. g. statutes, *court* decisions, regulations, news developments, etc.). However, in many of the services, the decisions appear only in a digested form.

2. Some unofficial topical reporters in particular fields will include both court decisions and administrative decisions. Examples of these are the *U. S. Patents Quarterly* which contain decisions of the federal courts

in patent matters, as well as selective decisions of the Commissioner of Patents and the Patent Office Board of Appeals; and *Public Utilities Reports*, which includes Federal Power Commission decisions, as well as court decisions in that field.

3.   Pike and Fischer's *Administrative Law Service* is devoted to *procedural* aspects of administrative law and contains decisions of the major regulatory agencies which have been rendered on questions of procedure. These are arranged according to the sections of the Federal Administrative Procedure Act, appearing first in looseleaf sheets, then in bound volumes.   The service also includes a digest, an index, court decisions, and rules of practice of some agencies.

CITATORS FOR FEDERAL ADMINISTRATIVE MATERIALS

Although Shepard's does not offer citator service for administrative *regulations*, it does include coverage of many important administrative agency *decisions*.   Since 1967 a separate citator was initiated for this purpose, *Shepard's United States Administrative Citations*.   Previously, many of those reports were included in *Shepard's U. S.* and *Federal Reporter Citations*.   In addition, administrative decisions in labor law are included in

Shepard's Labor Law Citations. There are also some other tools which perform a partial citator function. In summary, the following tools are useful in this area:

1. For Regulations:

    (a) Codification Guides in the *Federal Register.*

    (b) *Lists of Sections Affected* in *C.F.R.*

    (c) Looseleaf services in some fields.

    (d) Tables of Statutes Construed in *National Reporter System* and Lawyer's Co-op *Digest of U. S. Supreme Court Reports.*

    (e) Some regulations can be shepardized through their related federal statute citation.

2. For Decisions:

    (a) *Shepard's U. S. Administrative Citations.*

    (b) *Shepard's Labor Law Citations* for N.L.R.B. decisions.

    (c) Looseleaf services (particularly in taxation).

It is difficult to find citators for much of the federal administrative material, but on the state level, such aids are almost non-existent.

ADMINISTRATIVE LAW AT THE
STATE AND LOCAL LEVEL

On the state and local levels published administrative materials range from satisfactory sources in a few states to a great mass of inaccessible material in most states and localities. Since these administrative decrees may have the full force and sanction of law, their unavailability violates the fundamental principles of our legal system.

Although almost all states require the filing of administrative regulations with their secretary of state, few of these are compiled or published in anything like the *Federal Register* or *Code of Federal Regulations*. Most states provide only limited access to their regulations and decisions by request to particular agencies and do not offer a comprehensive collection in published form. Only eighteen states maintain current, well supplemented compilations of administrative regulations, while six states have no provision at all for either filing or publication.

With respect to the decisions and rulings of administrative agencies, the situation in the states is also disappointing. Many have published decisions of their public service commissions and some also issue the decisions of their taxation, labor, insurance and banking commissions, but for most other agencies, there is very little material available. A few looseleaf services, particularly in the taxation field, include decisions of state tribunals, but this practice does not extend to many fields.

On the municipal and local level, administrative decisions are almost never made public and regulations very rarely kept up to date. One would have to request a specific regulation from a town clerk or particular agency, if it were definitely known to exist. It would be very difficult, however, to determine the existence of a particular regulation since they are not available to the public in a compiled or current text, and are rarely indexed in their official files.

OPINIONS OF THE ATTORNEYS GENERAL

The opinions of the U. S. Attorney General and the attorneys general of the various states have considerable significance in legal research. These officials render formal and informal opinions of law in response to questions from their respective governments or officials. Their decisions are advisory in nature and do not have binding authority, but they are given considerable weight by the courts in interpreting statutes and regulations. Consequently they may be useful to the attorney with a similar problem or to the

scholar investigating that area of law. Most
states issue these opinions in bound volumes,
which are published chronologically. There
is usually an index in each volume, but these
rarely cumulate. In some states the opinions
are published every year, but in many there
is a long time lag between issuance and publication. These volumes are rarely preceded
by slip opinions.

For subject access to these rulings in all
of the states, the Council of State Governments formerly published the *Digest of Opinions of the Attorneys General*. Unfortunately, it stopped publication in 1969 and no other
service has replaced it.

There are now 41 volumes of the *Opinions
of the Attorney General of the United States*
and three cumulative digests, which provide
subject access to the first 32 volumes, that is
up to 1921. Opinions of the U. S. Attorney
General are listed in *Shepard's United States
Administrative Citations* and the opinions of
the attorneys general in ten of the states are
carried in their respective Shepard's citators.

Occasionally similar legal officials on the
local level will have their opinions published
and these provide useful sources of local
government law. The Opinions of the City
Solicitor of Philadelphia, which are published
annually, constitute one of the best of this
rare breed of publication.

CHAPTER VII

LOOSE-LEAF SERVICES

One of the unique inventions of legal bibliography has been the loose-leaf service, which offers researchers an easily supplemented tool in specific subject areas, containing legal source material of various kinds, special finding aids and secondary material. These publications provide *comprehensive, unified* and *current* access to selected fields of legal literature. They have become particularly popular in public law areas where government regulation is the central focus of legal development, e. g., taxation, labor, antitrust, and regulated industries such as transportation, communication, banking, utilities, etc. Recently new services have been published in such areas of current interest as environmental control, poverty law, urban law and education. For many lawyers specializing in those fields, the loose-leaf services define the parameters of their routine research.

The methods of organization of these tools will vary according to the nature of the material, the requirements of the subject matter, and the publisher's predilection. In areas where one major statute dominates the legal order, the services may be arranged by statutory sections or divisions (e. g. the taxation services, which are structured according to the sections of the Internal Revenue Code). Where several statutes are significant, the service may be divided into areas by the relevant statutes (e. g. labor law services which offer separate sections for the Labor Management Relations Act, the Labor Management Reporting and Disclosure Act, the Wage and Hour Act, State Laws, etc.). In other fields where common law or judicial rules predominate, or where there is a mixture of case and statutory law, the service may follow a logical arrangement of the subject matter (e. g. Trusts and Estates or Corporations).

ADVANTAGES

The advantages of loose-leaf services over separate research in each of the original primary sources are as follows:

1. Primary Sources Compiled. *All* relevant law is collected in one place by a convenient, compact, and coordinated presentation of primary authority, regardless of its original form of publication. By transcending the formal distinctions between varied legal sources, these services enable the researcher on a particular topic to do all or almost all of his work within the confines of a single tool. A lawyer can have available economically a wide range of material, which would otherwise require vast shelf space, greater costs and considerable searching and coordination.

A typical loose-leaf service may include the following *primary* sources:

(a) Statutes, both state and federal.

(b) Decisions, not only of state and federal *courts,* but also of administrative agencies which operate in that area.

(c) Rules and regulations of those administrative agencies, promulgated pursuant to their authorizing statute.

(d) Rulings of agencies on adjudicated matters or submitted questions.

Of course, each of these authorities would be available in its primary form of publication (e. g. in statutory compilations like the *U. S. Code* and similar state codes; in official and unofficial state and federal court reporters; in the *Federal Register,* the *Code of Federal Regulations* and state administrative compilations; and in the reporters of administrative agency decisions)—but, as noted above, at far greater cost in time, space and money.

2. Secondary Material. The aforesaid primary sources are collected and coordinated in the services with the following additional features:

(a) Summaries of proposed legislation and regulations, along with their analysis, status and purpose.

(b) News coverage of the legal and general developments in the particular area covered.

(c) Editorial notes and comments, interpretations of the primary sources, projections of current trends, and other secondary material.

3. Speed. By regular supplementation, all of these materials appear promptly, frequently weekly, while there are often delays in the *official* publication of the primary sources. The loose-leaf service cuts through these delays by offering prompt transmittals and an easy, economical means of updating by simply filing the new sheets into the service as they are received.

4. Integrated Coverage. The services cut across jurisdictional lines and cover their respective fields as units without regard to the source of the particular publications.

5. Indexing. Quick and detailed indexing, which coordinates the whole collection and affords convenient access at many points. A typical service may include all of the following indexes:

(a) **Rapid Finder Index**—using a broad, analytical approach, it divides the whole service into major areas and provides an initial orientation to its contents.

(b) **Basic Index**—using the catch word or topical approach, it provides more direct and specific reference to the service.

(c) **Finding Lists**—include different types of documentary material by their official citations; enabling the researcher to locate a specific regulation, rule, order, decision or ruling directly.

(d) **Current and Supplementary Indexes** —update the basic index and include the latest additions to the service.

(e) **Tables of Cases**—not only locate these materials directly (like the Finding Lists), but also provide a limited citator function.

COMMON FEATURES

A detailed and specific description of looseleaf services is impossible because of the variety and individuality of their form and content. Each publisher approaches the problem of arrangement in a slightly different way and the variations of subject material often require markedly different treatment as well. However, the following common features of most loose-leaf services can be noted:

1.   Loose-leaf supplementation by expandable binders into which sheets are filed periodically (weekly in the best services).

2.   Detailed instructions for use of the service, which are set out at the beginning of the first volume.

3.   Paragraph number arrangement and citation in preference to page references.

4.   Indexes and tables as described above.

5.   Current material and news developments.

6.   Commentary and editorial analysis on the primary sources.

RESEARCH STEPS IN USING SERVICES

Although again it is difficult to generalize about the best procedure to be followed in working with a loose-leaf service, the following steps are typical for most cases:

1.   Analysis of one's problem into general areas of concern, noting the type of source material likely to be needed.

2. Perusal of the instructions at the front of the applicable service, which, in three minutes, can usually provide an adequate working orientation. This is the most neglected step and one which can save the researcher much time and trouble.

3. Use of the service's various indexes to locate the specific material for solution of the problem—generally proceeding from the *Rapid Finder Index* to the *Basic Index* and then to the *Current Material Index.* If the researcher has specific reference to a relevant document (order, regulation, ruling or bulletin), he can use the *Finding Lists* to locate it directly.

4. Study of the actual texts of the relevant primary material, supplemented by the editorial explanation and secondary materials. It should be noted that, although many services contain only digests of court or administrative decisions, some will provide the *full* text of such decisions to subscribers on a complimentary basis, upon request.

5. Up-dating the relevant sources by use of the citators and current material sections.

TOPICAL REPORTERS

Many of the loose-leaf services also provide bound volumes for the permanent collection of court and administrative decisions in their fields. These decisions will have a continuing reference value and are to be retained despite changes in the rest of the service. In many cases, these unofficial reporters duplicate official editions (e. g. the *C.C.H.—N.L.R.B. Decisions* and the *B.N.A. Labor Relations Reference Manual* both include material which can be found in the official *Decisions of the National Labor Relations Board*). However, these reports include better indexing and finding devices than the official editions, are issued more quickly, and are tied into the other research features of their loose-leaf services.

CHAPTER VIII

U. S. TREATIES

Treaties are formal agreements between countries which have legal significance for both domestic and international purposes. Since Article VI of our Constitution provides that they shall be the supreme law of the land and shall bind all judges, treaties have the same legal effect and status as statutes. Treaties can supersede prior statutes and statutes can revoke prior treaties, as the Seneca Indians of New York discovered sadly a few years ago when their lands, secured to them for over 200 years by treaty, were taken from them pursuant to a later statute.

The treaties of the United States are published in a variety of forms—official and unofficial, national and international, current and retrospective. There are also several finding tools and aids available for research in treaties. Because some of the best publications in this area have been discontinued as the result of dubious government frugality, the bibliography of treaties remains varied and complex.

An understanding of treaty publications generally may be facilitated by a review of the following critical dates in the progress of a treaty from signing to adoption:

1. Date of Signing. The date on which the treaty is actually signed by the representatives of the U. S. and the other country is ordinarily used in citations. It is so cited by the Department of State and lawyers generally and is also the form of listing in *Shepard's Citations*. It is not, however, the treaty's effective date, nor the date on which it becomes the "Law of the Land".

2. Date of Approval by Senate. The date on which the Senate "consents" to the treaty by a two-thirds vote of those present.

3. Date of Ratification by the President.

4. Effective Date of Treaty. Unless the treaty provides otherwise, this is usually the date on which the President ratifies the treaty, or on which ratifications are exchanged with the other signatory.

5. Date of Proclamation. The date on which the President proclaims the treaty, following which it is usually published.

CURRENT PUBLICATION OF U. S. TREATIES AND EXECUTIVE AGREEMENTS

The following are the most common forms of treaty publication:

1. Press Releases of Department of State. These are usually issued on the date of signing—in mimeographed form.

2. Department of State Bulletin. This weekly periodical is an authoritative source of treaty information and usually contains the text of treaties shortly after signing. It also carries information concerning negotiations, congressional action, ratification, and other developments in the progress of the treaty from signing to proclamation.

3. Senate Executive Documents. A treaty is transmitted to the Senate for its consideration in this form. These publications usually include transmittal messages from the President and the Secretary of State. Sometimes Senate Executive Documents are initially confidential and are not available for distribution or listed in the *Monthly Catalog of U. S. Government Publications* until the Senate lifts its injunction of secrecy. They receive an *alphabetical* designation and are cited by that letter and by the number of the

[*169*]

Congress and session in which they are transmitted. They may be pending before the Senate for many sessions before approval, but still retain their original citation. Senate Executive Documents should be distinguished from Senate Executive Reports which contain the report of the Senate Committee on Foreign Relations on the treaty and receive a *numerical* designation. A useful bibliography of these documents and reports has been published by the Tarlton Law Library of the University of Texas: *Checklist of Senate Executive Documents and Reports. . . . 1947–1970* (December 1970), compiled by Mariana G. Mabry.

4. Slip Treaty Form. These publications are usually the first widely disseminated official publication and comprise the *Treaties and Other International Acts Series* (*T.I.A.S.*) which began in 1945, as a successor to two separate series called Treaty Series (1908–1945) and Executive Agreement Series (1929–1945). It is a pamphlet form of publication, similar to the statutory slip law. The slip treaties are cumulated and bound into the annual volumes of *United States Treaties and Other International Agreements*, but there is often a considerable delay between the effective date of a treaty and the publication of its slip form.

5. U. S. Treaties and Other International Agreements. Since 1949 when the publication of treaties in the *Statutes at Large* was discontinued, this series (*U.S.T.*) has become the permanent form of official treaty publication. These volumes cumulate the *T.I.A.S.* pamphlets in the same way that the *Statutes at Large* collect the slip laws. Several volumes are issued every year and each is indexed by subject and country. There is, however, no cumulative subject index to the whole set.

6. Unofficial Publications. There are some unofficial sources for U. S. treaties, but they are selective and do not offer the complete coverage of *T.I.A.S.* and *U.S.T.* *U.S.C.A.*, like the *U. S. Code* itself, publishes a few important treaties which substantially affect related Code provisions (e. g. the Universal Copyright Convention in Title 17). *CCH Tax Treaties* is a loose-leaf service which publishes treaties relating to federal taxation.

7. United Nations Treaty Series. Since 1946 this series has published all treaties registered with the United Nations by member nations (including the U. S.) and some filed by non-members. It succeeds the old *League of Nations Treaty Series* which was published on a similar basis from 1920 to 1945. The treaties appear in their original

languages *and* in English and French translations. Cumulative indexes originally appeared for each one hundred volumes published
and more recently for every fifty volumes.
The series is the most comprehensive treaty
collection and already contains over 630 volumes. Similar series of their own treaties
are published by some individual countries
and regional organizations.

RETROSPECTIVE COLLECTIONS
OF U. S. TREATIES

For research in treaties of the past, the
following historical sources are generally
used:

1. Indian Treaties. Vol. 7 of the
Statutes at Large included a collection of
Indian treaties for the years 1778–1842.
Thereafter, Indian Treaties continued to ap-
pear with other treaties in the regular vol-
umes of the *Statutes at Large.* The best com-
pilations of Indian Treaties (and statutes)—
are Kappler, *Indian Affairs, Laws and
Treaties* (U.S.G.P.O., 1904–1941, 5 vols.), Fe-
lix Cohen's *Handbook of Federal Indian Law*
(U.S.G.P.O., 1945) and *Federal Indian Law*
(U.S.G.P.O., 1958).

2. Statutes at Large. Vol. 8 of the
Statutes at Large published a compilation of

treaties entered into between 1778 and 1845; and thereafter, until 1949, treaties appeared regularly in the individual volumes of *Statutes*. Volume 18 includes a collection of treaties in force as of 1873 and was published in connection with the *Revised Statutes of 1873*. Beginning in 1931 executive international agreements were also included. In 1949 both of these were discontinued and the *U.S.T.* took over the publication of both treaties and agreements. The last volume of the *Statutes at Large* to include treaties (vol. 64) also included a complete listing of all treaties appearing in the *Statutes*, arranged by country.

3. Malloy's Treaties, Conventions, International Acts, Protocols and Agreements between the U.S.A. and Other Powers (U.S.G. P.O., 1910–1938, 4 vols.). *Malloy* has been one of the most useful retrospective collections of U. S. treaties. Volumes 1 and 2 cover the period from 1776 to 1909; Vol. 3 by C. F. Redmond (often cited as 3 *Redmond*) covers 1910 to 1923; and Vol. 4 by E. J. Trenwith (often cited as 4 *Trenwith*) covers 1923–1937. These volumes include only the English text. The last volume includes a very useful cumulative subject index covering the whole period, 1776 to 1937; a chronological list of treaties; a list by country; and a list of all treaties submitted to the Senate during that period with the Senate's actions thereon noted.

4. Miller's Treaties and Other International Acts of the U.S.A. (U.S.G.P.O., 1931–1948, 9 Vols.). This valuable compilation, issued by the State Department, covers the period from 1776 to 1863. Its scholarly notes and annotations promised to make it even more important than *Malloy*, but it was unfortunately discontinued by the State Department for lack of funds in 1948. For the period covered it is still a very useful research tool. The arrangement is chronological and it suffers from the lack of an index.

5. Bevans' Treaties and Other International Agreements of the United States of America 1776–1949 (U.S.G.P.O., 1968–). This new retrospective compilation of American treaties is designed to bring together in a convenient form all treaties and other international agreements entered into by the United States from 1776 to 1949. It is predicted that the set will comprise 15 volumes, the first 4 of which will contain multilateral treaties (arranged chronologically by date of signature) and the balance, bilateral treaties (arranged alphabetically by countries). Cumulative analytical indexes are promised and when completed, the set will replace *Mal-*

loy and become the definitive retrospective compilation.

6. League of Nations Treaty Series. Although not a member of the League, U. S. treaties appeared in this series during its publication from 1920 to 1946. It is now discontinued, having been succeeded by the *United Nations Treaty Series*, as noted above, but it is still the best collection for the period covered.

7. Consolidated Treaty Series (Oceana, 1969–). Designed to include every treaty between national states from 1641 to 1918, this new series will also include treaties of the United States prior to the *League of Nations Treaty Series*.

FINDING TOOLS

Because of the chronological publication of treaties and the necessity for some means of subject access to them, the following finding tools are generally used:

1. Treaties in Force. The most important current index to United States treaties in force is this annual publication of the Department of State, which has been issued since 1950. It is revised annually to include only treaties *in force,* but gives citations to earlier forms of such treaties where appropriate. It offers citations to all of the treaty publications—*Bevans, League of Nations Treaty Series, Malloy, Miller, Statutes at Large, T.I.A.S., U. N. Treaty Series* and *U.S.T.* The first part of the index lists bilateral treaties alphabetically by country and then subdivides them by subject. The second section lists multilateral treaties alphabetically by subject. This index is usually the starting point for searching current treaties. Its two sections are illustrated in Exhibit 38 below. Unfortunately, treaty research is handicapped by the lack of an overall index to *all* U. S. treaties in force arranged by subject.

2. Multilateral Treaties in Respect of Which the Secretary General Performs Depositary Functions (United Nations, Office of Legal Affairs). This useful compilation supersedes the *United Nations Status of Multilateral Conventions*. It consists of two volumes, the first is to be an annually revised, comprehensive list of multilateral treaties arranged by subject with current information as to their status, signatories, ratifications, accessions, etc. It will also include, for the first time, coverage of League of Nations multilateral treaties. The second volume is an annex giving the final clauses of such treaties, issued in looseleaf form to permit convenient updating. The new format and

ALBANIA

EXTRADITION
   Treaty of extradition.
   Signed at Tirana March 1, 1933; entered
   into force November 14, 1935.
   49 Stat. 3313; TS 902; IV Trenwith 3923;
   166 LNTS 195.

NATIONALITY
   Treaty of naturalization.
   Signed at Tirana April 5, 1932; entered
   into force July 22, 1935.
   49 Stat. 3241; TS 892; IV Trenwith 3922;
   162 LNTS 31.

PACIFIC SETTLEMENT OF DISPUTES
   Arbitration treaty.
   Signed at Washington October 22, 1928;
   entered into force February 12, 1929.
   45 Stat. 2728; TS 770; IV Trenwith 3919;
   92 LNTS 217.

   Treaty of conciliation.
   Signed at Washington October 22, 1928;
   entered into force February 12, 1929.
   45 Stat. 2732; TS 771; IV Trenwith 3920;
   92 LNTS 223.

POSTAL MATTERS
   Convention for the exchange of money
   orders.
   Signed at Washington June 18, 1932;
   entered into force October 1, 1932.

TRADE AND COMMERCE
   Agreement concerning most-favored-
   nation treatment and passports.
   Exchange of notes at Tirana June 23
   and 25, 1922; operative July 28, 1922.
   Foreign Relations, 1925, Vol. I, p. 511.

VISAS
   Agreement relating to waiver of passport
   visa fees for nonimmigrants.
   Exchange of notes at Tirana May 7, 1926;
   operative June 1, 1926.

EXTRADITION

Convention on extradition.
Signed at Montevideo December 26, 1933;
entered into force for the United States
January 25, 1935.
49 Stat. 3111; TS 882; IV Trenwith 4800;
165 LNTS 45.
States which are parties:

Argentina	Guatemala
Chile[1]	Honduras[1]
Colombia	Mexico[1]
Dominican Republic	Nicaragua
Ecuador[1]	Panama
El Salvador[1]	United States[2]

FINANCE (See also REPARATIONS)

Articles of agreement of the International
Monetary Fund, formulated at the Bretton
Woods Conference July 1 - 22, 1944.[3]
Opened for signature at Washington
December 27, 1945; entered into force for
the United States December 27, 1945.
60 Stat. 1401; TIAS 1501; 2 UNTS 39.
States which are parties:

Afghanistan	Ethiopia
Argentina	Finland
Australia	France
Austria	Germany, Fed. Rep.
Belgium	Ghana
Bolivia	Greece
Brazil	Guatemala
Burma	Haiti
Canada	Honduras
Ceylon	Iceland
Chile	India
China	Indonesia
Colombia	Iran
Costa Rica	Iraq
Cuba	Ireland
Cyprus	Israel
Denmark	Italy
Dominican Republic	Japan
Ecuador	Jordan
El Salvador	Korea

---

[1] With reservation.

[2] With an understanding.

[3] Applicable to all territories.

Exhibit 38:   *Treaties in Force.*   Bilateral treaties on
                the left (arranged by country and then
                subject);   multilateral treaties on the
                right (listed by subject).

improved supplementation should make this
a much more valuable reference tool.

**3. Status of Inter-American Treaties and
Conventions (Pan American Union).** This
annual status table offers substantially the

same data on Pan American treaties as does the United Nations service described above.

4.   Indexes to the United Nations Treaty Series.   These indexes cover many more treaties than those of the United States.   As noted above, they now cumulate every fifty volumes and are essential for research in the *United Nations Treaty Series.*   The researcher should note that these indexes are not limited to treaties in force and may refer to treaties which have been modified or renounced.

GUIDES TO THE LEGISLATIVE HISTORY OF TREATIES

Congressional deliberations and actions on pending treaties, like the legislative histories of statutes, are often the subject of legal research.   The following finding tools aid in locating relevant material:

1.   CCH Congressional Index.   This looseleaf service, discussed above in Chapter V, includes among its other features a table of treaties pending before the Senate.   It is the single most valuable status table for determining actions taken on pending treaties and their present status, regardless of when they were introduced.   Treaty listings include references to Executive Reports of the Senate Foreign Relations Committee, hearings, ratifications, etc.   The treaties are listed chronologically by the session of transmittal and designated by their executive letter. The table is shown in Exhibit 39, below:

EXECUTIVE K
88th Cong.—1st Sess.
FORCED LABOR

Convention concerning Abolition of Forced Labor, adopted by International Labor Conference at its 40th session on June 25, 1957.

Injunction of secrecy removed July 22, 1963.

In S. Foreign Relations Committee.

Hearing, February 23, 1967.

Hearing available, April 21, 1967.

Hearing, September 13, 1967.

Hearing available, October 24, 1967.

EXECUTIVE L
88th Cong.—1st Sess.
ABOLITION OF SLAVERY

Supplementary Convention on the Abolition of Slavery, signed at Geneva on September 7, 1956.

Injunction of secrecy removed July 22, 1963.

In S. Foreign Relations Committee.

Hearing, September 13, 1967.

Hearing available, October 24, 1967.

Committee Executive Rept. No. 16, October 31, 1967.

Convention ratified by S. [Roll-call], November 2, 1967.

EXECUTIVE D.
88th Cong.—2d Sess.
CONSULAR CONVENTION—USSR

Consular convention and related protocol with the Union of Soviet Socialist Republics, signed at Moscow June 1, 1964.

Exhibit 39: An entry from the *CCH Congressional Index* table of treaties pending before the Senate.

2.   Calendar of the Senate Foreign Relations Committee.   This official status table of business before the Senate committee is perhaps the best list of pending treaties with actions taken thereon, but has been less accessible than the CCH service.   Its information on hearings is particularly useful.

3.   Congressional Information Service.   This new service, described earlier, includes coverage of treaties.   These appear in the subject index, documents lists and in the summaries of actions by committee.

4.   Congressional Quarterly.   This service, which is devoted to congressional activity generally, also includes useful information on treaties.   In addition to occasional special reports on major treaties, the *Weekly Report* of *C.Q.* includes the actual text of important documents, chronologies, summaries of debates and messages, and general information about current treaties.   The indexes to the *Weekly Reports* offer leads to current information and documents on pending treaties.

5.   Congressional Record Indexes.   In the fortnightly indexes to the *Congressional Record* and in the bound volume index for each session there is a listing of treaty actions and discussions appearing in the *Record*.   These references appear under the heading "Treaties" in the alphabetical subject index and also occasionally under the name of a particular treaty or its subject matter. The *Congressional Record* indexes are not very convenient for current use, but they are helpful for retrospective research into a particular treaty's legislative history. However, they only cover material in the *Record,* which is not the only source of legislative history of treaties.

6. Lists of Treaties Submitted to the Senate. The Department of State has issued treaty lists of different kinds, among which are the following three lists of treaties submitted to the Senate:

> *List of Treaties Submitted to Senate, 1789–1931, which have not gone into Force* (Publication No. 382, 1932).
>
> *List of Treaties Submitted to the Senate, 1789–1934* (Publication No. 765, 1935).
>
> *Treaties Submitted to the Senate, 1935–1944* (Publication No. 2311, 1945).

Although long out of date, these publications are still used, particularly in historical studies of legislative action on treaties.

7. Senate Committee on Foreign Relations Reports, 1789–1901 (Senate Doc. 231, 56th Congress, 2nd session, in 8 volumes). Although not a guide to legislative history, this set is a handy compilation of important source material for that purpose. It is an exhaustive collection of regular committee reports, executive reports and documents. There is a cumulative index in the last volume.

EXTRINSIC AIDS IN TREATY RESEARCH

The study of treaties often involves their history and interpretation, for which the following external sources may offer useful information:

1. Citators. The interpretation of treaties by courts provides authoritative material for the researcher who seeks information on the meaning or effect of a treaty. Citations to such decisions can be found in:

(a) **Shepard's United States Citations— Statutes Edition.** Limited to *federal* court decisions, but includes all cases mentioning the treaty in addition to those actually interpreting it. For treaties up to 1949, listing is by date of signing rather than by *Statutes at Large* citation. After 1950 a special section was set up listing treaties by their treaty series citation. Shepard's also includes modifications of the cited treaty by later legislation or a subsequent treaty change.

(b) **Shepard's Citations for various states.** There are similar listings of state court decisions citing U. S. treaties in the statutes volume of every state Shepard's Citator. Many more judicial interpretations of U. S. treaties occur in the *state* courts than in the federal courts.

(c) **Federal Code Annotated.** In a special volume of *Annotations to Uncodified Laws & Treaties,* this edition of the *United States Code* includes citations to both state and federal judicial decisions interpreting U. S. treaties.

(d) **Digest of U. S. Supreme Court Reports** (Lawyers Co-op.). Volume 14 of this Digest lists U. S. Supreme Court decisions citing and construing treaties, including some of which the United States was not a signatory. The listing is both chronological and alphabetical by country.

(e) **American International Law Cases.** (Oceana). Edited by Francis Deak, this series, planned for publication in 1971, will include American federal and state court decisions from 1783 to 1968. The set will include annotations, where appropriate, to relevant treaties.

2. Digests of International Law. There have been a number of encyclopedic digests of international law which include material on treaties and their judicial interpretation, analytical and historic notes, and other scholarly comments. These include:

(a) Cadwalader, John L. *Digest of the Published Opinions of the Attorney General and of Leading Decisions of the Federal Courts, with Reference to International Law, Treaties and Kindred Subjects* (1877).

(b) Wharton, Francis. *A Digest of the International Law of the United States* (1886 in 3 volumes and 2nd ed. in 1887 with appendix). Continued and expanded Cadwalader's Digest.

(c) Moore, John Bassett. *A Digest of International Law* (1906 in 8 volumes). Largely superseded Wharton.

(d) Hackworth, Green H. *Digest of International Law* (1940–44 in 8 volumes). Based on material which developed since Moore, but does not entirely supersede it.

(e) Whiteman, Marjorie M. *Digest of International Law* (1963–date, partially published, balance in preparation). Succeeds Hackworth, but does not replace it.

CHAPTER IX

SECONDARY MATERIALS

Most of the materials discussed so far have been primary sources of law, that is documents with actual legal effect (reports, statutes, regulations, treaties, etc.) or their related bibliographic apparatus (digests, indexes, citators, etc.). Primary materials may have mandatory or persuasive authority (or no authority at all) depending on their source, official status and inherent quality, the jurisdiction and tribunal in which they are presented, and their legal and factual relevance to a particular problem. We now examine the vast literature of unofficial, non-authoritative, *secondary* materials consisting of encyclopedias, treatises, periodicals and related publications. These range from scholarly writings of the highest repute and lasting influence through a varied spectrum down to hack work of low quality and fortunately short life. When creatively and effectively exploited, the best of the secondary materials may directly affect the development of the law. Many scholarly articles have shaped law reform and stimulated new legislation (e. g. Erwin Griswold's article, *Government in Ignorance of the Law—A Plea for Better Publication of Executive Leg-*

islation, appearing in the Harvard Law Review in 1934, which had considerable influence in bringing about the passage of the Federal Register Act of 1935).

Secondary materials also perform other more mundane functions in legal research. They serve as search books or finding tools which aid the researcher to locate relevant primary sources and authorities. They can refresh the reader's recollection of a well settled, but neglected area, or introduce him to the state of the law in a newly developing field. Handbooks and manuals provide the forms and guidelines for the operational details of daily law practice. From other sources, the lawyer or scholar can construct or buttress legal arguments and enhance his advocacy. Some works may describe the non-legal context or historical background of a legally significant event or state of affairs, while others illuminate the possible effects and social consequences of proposed legal action. Creative insights can reveal trends and patterns in unsettled areas and detect incipient strains and shifts in apparently settled law.

Although secondary materials are as old as legal research, they have been used and cited more frequently in recent years by both lawyers and judges to bring non-legal scholarship to bear on legal problems. A greater interest in the social and economic consequences of particular legal actions has led to interdisciplinary cooperation between law and the other social sciences. The development of social and experimental schools of jurisprudence further enhanced this interest in materials which are available only in secondary sources. The extension of legal concern into many new areas of human activity and the growing willingness of the courts to re-examine and revise traditional notions have increased the importance of secondary materials (viz. recent developments in the areas of criminal law, civil rights, reapportionment, etc.). Judicial and legislative history of recent years contains a scholarly documentation far more eclectic than the strictly legal references of the older literature.

The means of access to secondary sources vary widely. Some, like the encyclopedias, *Restatements of Law* and treatises, are in effect self-indexing. Periodicals are accessible through separate tools, such as the *Index to Legal Periodicals*. Separately published books and non-serial publications can be identified and retrieved through several bibliographic guides (e. g. *Law Books in Print)* and, of course, the card catalogs of many libraries.

LEGAL ENCYCLOPEDIAS

Although legal encyclopedias are avidly used by unsophisticated law students and many lawyers, they are considered by many neither very scholarly nor authoritative. Among academics, they lack the prestige of general encyclopedias like the older *Britannicas* or the *Encyclopedia of Social Sciences*. If, however, they are not used as authority in their own right, but rather as finding tools to the primary sources of authority, they can be helpful aids to legal research. Although their use requires more caution than novices are likely to exercise, they need not be totally avoided, as some law professors would suggest. In any case, encyclopedias are widely used (and often misused), particularly in smaller towns and rural areas where full law libraries may not be available. Because of their convenience and the apparent completeness of their predigested research, they will undoubtedly continue to flourish.

The two main legal encyclopedias are *Corpus Juris Secundum,* published by the West Publishing Company, and *American Jurisprudence 2nd,* published by Lawyers' Co-operative Publishing Company. Both employ an alphabetical arrangement of broad legal topics similar to those of the digests and provide indexing both to the entire set and to individual topics. The articles are prepared by editorial writers of each publisher and are not generally farmed out to legal scholars. The legal propositions and discussions are supported by extensive footnotes containing hundreds of citations to relevant and not so relevant judicial decisions. These footnotes give the encyclopedias their value as search books, described more fully in Chapter III above.

Although encyclopedias are often quoted for axiomatic statements of broadly accepted law, their texts lack the careful analysis and fine distinctions of a good treatise. Although both *C.J.S.* and *Am.Jur.* (as they are called) are supplemented by annual pocket parts and completely revised every generation, they are often slow to reflect subtle changes in the law and significant trends which might be apparent to the alert scholar. Other shortcomings include both gaps and overlapping between articles; overgeneralization and oversimplification; neglect of statutory law and almost complete reliance on case law. This last factor results in a grossly misleading view of our law, in which statutes bulk quite large.

Not surprisingly, each encyclopedia emphasizes the sister publications of its respective publisher. *Corpus Juris Secundum* purports to cite in its footnotes all of the significant decisions found in the West digests, while *American Jurisprudence* provides similar leads in its references to the numerous annotations of *A.L.R.* Both West and Lawyers Co-op also publish several state encyclopedias which follow roughly the same pattern as their national publications. In addition, there are a number of topical encyclopedias covering specific subjects in depth, with an appeal to practitioners and researchers in those particular areas.

Words and Phrases, also described and illustrated in Chapter III, can be mentioned here as an encyclopedic collection of legally significant words and phrases. These are arranged alphabetically, with numerous constructions, interpretations and definitions culled from the cases reported in the *National Reporter System* and West's federal reporters. If one's research focuses on the meaning of a particular word or phrase, this set is a very useful source of judicial interpretations. It is kept up to date by annual pocket parts, as well as by tables of words and phrases appearing in the advance sheets and bound volumes of the West reporters.

TEXTS AND TREATISES

In addition to the encyclopedias, there are thousands of texts and treatises dealing with the many topics of substantive and procedural law. These include multi-volume topical encyclopedias and detailed surveys, as well as short monographs on limited aspects of single topics. Legal treatises appeared shortly after the earliest English reports in the 12th century *Plea Rolls*. They summarized the developing law of the English courts and statutes and contributed their own analysis and influence to this development. One of the first and most durable of these treatises was that of Henry Bracton which appeared around 1250. Bracton stated his intent most felicitously in the following language, which describes as well the purpose of many later serious commentators (as translated by Pound and Plucknett in their *Readings in the History of the Common Law,* Lawyers Co-op, 3rd ed.1927, p. 127–8):

"Since, however, laws and customs of this kind are often abusively perverted by the foolish and unlearned (who ascend the judgment-seat before they have learnt the laws), and those who are involved in doubts and conjectures are very frequently led astray by their elders, who decide causes rather according to their own pleasure than by the authority of the laws, I, Henry de Bracton, have, for the instruction, at least of the younger generation, undertaken the task of diligently examining the ancient judgments of righteous men, not without much loss of sleep and labour, and by reducing their acts, counsels, and answers, and whatever thereof I have found noteworthy into one summary, I have brought it into order under titles and paragraphs (without prejudice against any better system) to be commended to perpetual memory by the aid of writing; requesting the reader, if he should find anything superfluous or erroneously stated in this work, to correct and amend it, or to pass it over with eyes half closed, since to retain everything in memory, and to make no mistakes, is an attribute of God rather than man."

Legal texts and treatises, like encyclopedias, lack authority and legal effect and are never *binding* on courts. Some of them, however, are written by scholars of outstanding reputation and prestige and hence engender considerable judicial respect. Other texts make no pretense at scholarly analysis but offer convenient guides in which practitioners can familiarize themselves with particular fields of law. These practice books often contain sample forms, checklists and how-to-do-it advice.   Among the varied types of texts, the following groups can be noted:

1. Scholarly surveys of particular fields in depth (e. g. Wigmore on Evidence, Corbin on Contracts).

2. Hornbooks, student texts and treatise abridgements (e. g. Prosser on Torts, Simpson on Contracts.)

3. Practitioners' handbooks in particular fields.

4. Procedural manuals (e. g. Goodrich-Amram *Standard Pennsylvania Practice*).

5. Specialized monographs on more or less narrow topics.

6. Comprehensive commentaries, histories and works of jurisprudence (e. g. Blackstone's *Commentaries*, Pound's *Jurisprudence*, Holdsworth's *History of English Law*).

These works may be supplemented by loose-leaf inserts, pocket parts or bound additions. *Some* form of up-dating is usually essential however, and works which are not supplemented lose their value as to current law coverage very quickly.   The bypaths of legal bibliography are cluttered with the debris of out-dated, but unrevised texts.   The ever-changing nature of law requires a literature capable of reflecting that change promptly and accurately.

It is often difficult for the researcher to evaluate texts, but the following considerations may aid selection from among the many available: the purpose of the particular publication; the reputation of the author and publisher and the standing of their previous books; the organization, scope and depth of research in this work; its scholarly apparatus (footnotes, tables, bibliography, etc.); the adequacy of supplementation and present timeliness; and how it has been reviewed.

RESTATEMENTS OF THE LAW

Some of the most important commentaries on American law are to be found in the series of *Restatements* prepared and published during the last 30 years under the auspices of the American Law Institute. These surveys of particular legal subjects were designed:

"To present an orderly restatement of the general common law of the United States, including in that term not only the law developed solely by judicial decision, but also law that has grown from the application by the courts of statutes that were generally enacted and were in force for many years."

They cover many, but not all, of the important fields, including contracts, torts, agency, trusts, etc. In most cases a second edition of the *Restatement* has been or is being prepared to reflect new developments or later thinking. While these revisions are being drafted and debated, tentative drafts of their sections are distributed and are of considerable interest to scholars and researchers.

The *Restatements* are divided into sections, each of which contains a "black letter" general statement of law, followed by an explanatory comment on the general principles, and then illustrated by examples of particular cases and variations on the general proposition. A general index volume is provided for all of the *Restatements*, as well as individual indexes for each subject. A glossary of terms defines the significant words appearing in the *Restatements*.

Separate volumes of annotations of court decisions citing or applying the various *Restatement* sections have been provided for many of the states. Supplementary volumes of the *Restatements in the Courts* have been issued for the same purpose. *Shepard's Citations* also include the *Restatements* and list court decisions in many jurisdictions citing sections of the various *Restatements*.

Although they are not official and are not binding, the *Restatements* are persuasive in the courts—perhaps more so than any other

[*196*]

secondary material. Their authors, advisors and discussants are well known scholars and include outstanding members of the judiciary. Although some of the reporters reflected what they thought the law ought to be rather than what the law was, by and large these volumes are considered among the authoritative works of American legal scholarship. Model codes have also been prepared as part of the same overall project and some like the recently approved *Model Penal Code* are already influencing new legislation.

PERIODICALS

American legal periodicals parallel in quality and variety the other secondary materials. They have been said to reflect "the law as it was, as it is, as it is tending, and as it ought to be". Periodicals are issued by law schools, bar associations, private publishers, and other groups. Their source is often indicative of their quality and point of view, the most scholarly being the student-edited law school reviews, which are published by every major law school as a training ground for their best students. They contain articles by established scholars, student comments and case notes, which reflect change and innovation in the law, as well as describe historical developments, and mirror the current state of the law. Outstanding articles in the best reviews are often persuasive in the courts and are occasionally cited in judicial opinions.

1. Types of Periodicals. Examples of the varied types of legal periodicals include the following:

(a) Law school reviews for almost every accredited school.

(b) Specialized scholarly journals like *Law and Contemporary Problems, Journal of Family Law, Tax Law Review* and *American Journal of Legal History.*

(c) Bar association journals, including those national in scope like the *American Bar Association Journal*; state-wide like the *Pennsylvania Bar Association Quarterly* and *New York State Bar Bulletin*; local like the Philadelphia Bar Association's *Shingle* and the *Record* of the Association of the Bar of the City of New York; and those of professionally specialized bar groups like the *I.C.C. Practitioners' Journal* and the *Journal of the Patent Office Society.*

(d) Commercial journals in specialized fields like CCH's *Insurance Law Journal, Labor Law Journal,* etc.

[*198*]

(e) Legal newspapers in many large cities, such as the *New York Law Journal, Philadelphia Legal Intelligencer,* etc.

2. Periodical Indexes. Access to this huge periodical literature is provided by the following indexes, most of which are similar to those in other fields:

(a) Jones-Chipman Index to *Periodical Literature* (1803–1937).

(b) *Index to Legal Periodicals* (1926-to date)—3 year cumulations, annual supplements, monthly advance sheets (except for September).

—Indexes by author, subject, cases, book reviews.

—Scope: approximately 300 periodicals.

(c) *Index to Foreign Legal Periodicals and Collections of Essays* (1960 to date)

—Quarterly pamphlets, annual volumes and 3 year cumulations.

—Coverage: Articles and book reviews and, since 1963, collections of essays, bibliographies, biographies and Festschriften.

—Subject and author indexes, geographic index and book review index.

—Scope: 260 periodicals.

(d) *Harvard Current and Annual Legal Bibliography*

—Monthly pamphlets (except for July –September) and annual volumes.

—Coverage: Periodicals, books, essays (American and foreign).

—Classified arrangement by subject and country.

(e) *Index to Periodical Articles Related to Law*

—Coverage: Journals not included in the *Index to Legal Periodicals* or the *Index to Foreign Legal Periodicals*.

—Quarterly with annual cumulations and ten year cumulation (1970).

(f) *Current Index to Legal Periodicals* (University of Washington Law Library and Washington Law Review)— Weekly subject guide to the contents of law school reviews and other major legal periodicals.

(g) *Periodical digests*:

—*CCH Federal Tax Articles* (monthly supplementation)

—*Law Review Digest* (bimonthly)

3.   Periodical Citator. Shepard's Citations publishes the *Shepard's Law Review Citations,* a compilation of citations to articles in over 140 law reviews and legal periodicals. This citator will permit the user to determine where any article published since 1947 has been cited in later articles from 1957 to date, or in state or federal decisions.

SPECIAL MATERIALS

There are a number of other specialized types of secondary material which should also be noted:

1. Directories of practicing lawyers are published, which are based on professional specialization, geographical area, or bar association membership. The most comprehensive of these is *Martindale-Hubbell* which provides a national listing of lawyers in all states, most cities and many towns. The first four volumes of *Martindale-Hubbell* provide classified listings, as well as fuller descriptions of those who care to purchase space beyond a simple one line entry. In addition, the fifth volume of the directory includes court calendars and brief digests of the law of every state and many foreign countries on specific legal topics. These are usually prepared by outstanding practitioners in the area and often provide references to the primary sources on which they are based. Although they are no substitute for actual research in the authoritative sources and cannot support a definitive judgment, they are useful for a brief statement of law on a particular point or for a reference from which further research can be undertaken.

2. Records and Briefs. The printed records and briefs of the parties in cases before appellate courts are distributed to a limited number of libraries around the country for future reference use. The records and briefs of the Supreme Court of the United States, in their official form, go to approximately 25 libraries around the country, while another 40 libraries subscribe to a microcard edition. Records and briefs of the various U. S. Courts of Appeals have a similar but more limited distribution. Records and briefs of the appellate courts in most states are also distributed. These materials have a permanent value in that they enable attorneys and other legal researchers to study in detail the arguments and facts of particularly significant cases decided by these courts. These documents are usually retrievable by the report citation or docket number of the original case in which they were submitted. The researcher must begin with an interest in a case or decision and then seek this additional source of material on the case. There is no direct subject approach to appellate records and briefs. The record consists of a transcript of all proceedings below, including the trial testimony, as well as all of the previous legal papers, documents, opinions and judgments. The briefs consist of the written arguments and authorities cited by the attorneys for the respective parties.

3. Form Books. Because of the recurrence of similar problems in the course of legal practice, a literature of form books has developed which contains sample forms of commonly used legal documents and instruments. These can be consulted by attorneys and used as the basis for the preparation of similar papers in later situations. Forms can be found in great multi-volumed collections covering different types of proceedings and subjects and as singly printed forms for a particular transaction or purpose which can be purchased at a legal stationery store. In between are handbooks or manuals of practice in particular subject areas, statutory forms which are often issued in conjunction with a state statutory compilation, and annotated form books which include citations to cases wherein the particular forms have actually been litigated and upheld on appeal.

4. Bar Associations issue legal materials of various kinds including the following types of publication:

(a) Newsletters and periodicals containing reports on association activities, arti-

cles on legal topics, and notices of recent developments.

(b) Annual proceedings or yearbooks of
meetings and committee reports.

(c) Handbooks or manuals for the continuing legal education of practitioners.

(d) Comments or special reports on proposed legislation or important developments in law.

There are many, many other types of secondary materials, but these are perhaps the
most important.   Modern legal research involves a great variety of sources, legal and
non-legal, although the confines of this *Nutshell* are quite limited.

CHAPTER X

FOREIGN AND INTERNA-
TIONAL LAW

Although this is primarily a manual of *American* legal bibliography, some mention might appropriately be made of the main sources of international law and of the law of foreign countries, both of which are of increasing importance in our own legal system. We have mentioned our English antecedents at several points, but more is undoubtedly necessary. Our historical nexus and continuing mutual interests justify fuller attention to the sources of English law. Each of the three topics discussed below (*International, Foreign* and *English Law*) obviously deserves fuller coverage than can be given in this sketchy outline, but even this brief treatment may be of some help to the novice.

INTERNATIONAL LAW

1. Introduction. International law is the law governing relations between nations—it is to be distinguished from foreign law, which refers to the domestic law of nations other than our own. Simply stated, international law deals with the external relations of nations, while foreign law refers to the internal law governing matters *within* a particular country.

International law can be viewed as those rules, procedures and customs which regulate the conduct of nations in their relations with each other. Its literature includes the following sources:

(a) Traditional law of nations

(b) Treaties, covenants and agreements between nations

(c) Classical commentators and digests on international law

(d) International adjudications, tribunals and arbitrations

(e) Law developed by international organizations

(f) Law of foreign relations (including diplomatic and consular law)

(g) Municipal law of individual states relating to international matters

Most of these sources lie within the broad bibliographic categories already discussed. Treatises, casebooks, encyclopedias and digests are available for basic research in these areas of international law. The specialized literature of international organizations may require special attention, however.

2. International Organizations. Today international organizations, like the United

Nations and the European Economic Community, are a major source of international law. Research in their documents and in the general literature about them is becoming increasingly frequent in American law libraries.

In beginning work on a current problem dealing with an international organization or its activities, it is often useful to begin with the yearbooks of that organization, particularly if the primary documents of the organization are not easily accessible. These yearbooks review the activities of the organization during the preceding year and frequently provide general directory information. The existence of a relevant yearbook can be ascertained from the *Yearbook of International Organizations* which provides data on all international organizations. If a yearbook has been located, its index will provide access to pertinent information. These volumes also have a permanent reference value, since research can be carried out retrospectively in their review sections, and citations to primary sources and documents can be found in them. Among the most useful are the following:

(a) *Yearbook of International Organizations* (Brussels, Union of International Associations, 1951 to date, published every two years in English)

(b) *Yearbook of the United Nations* (United Nations, 1946–7–)

(c) *Yearbook on Human Rights* (United Nations, 1946–)

(d) *Yearbook of the European Convention on Human Rights* (The European Commission and European Court of Human Rights, 1955–56–57–)

(e) *Yearbook of the International Court of Justice* (1946–7–)

(f) *United Nations Juridical Yearbook* (United Nations, 1963–)

(g) *Yearbook of the International Law Commission* (United Nations, 1949—)

(h) *European Yearbook (Annuaire Européen)*—published under the auspices of the Council of Europe annually at the Hague, 1955 to date, with coverage of several European organizations.

(i) *Everyman's United Nations*—an invaluable basic reference tool on all phases of the U. N. and related organizations—similar to the U. S. *Government Organization Manual,* but not issued annually (United Nations, latest edition: 1968).

3. Bibliographic Guides to International Organizations. The publications of the United Nations are probably the most important materials in the field of international organizations and, because of their rapid growth and diverse sources, they are the most complex. The following indexes and guides are particularly useful in locating specific documents or developing research leads:

(a) *United Nations Documents Index* (Vol. 1, 1950—to date). This is the single most important finding tool for U. N. documents. It is issued monthly with a cumulative annual index and checklist, listing all documents and publications, except restricted and internal papers. It is similar to our *Monthly Catalog of U. S. Government Publications* and includes two separate sections: a checklist arranged by agency and series, and a subject index.

(b) *Checklists of United Nations Documents (1946–49)*—This is a special series listing documents of all U. N. organs, issued prior to the *United Nations Documents Index*, with subject indexes.

(c) *United Nations Publications, 1967* (with periodic supplements and revisions). Although basically a sales catalog, this is also a useful and comprehensive guide to U. N. publications.

There are similar catalogs for other related organizations.

(d) Brimmer, et al. *A Guide to the Use of United Nations Documents* (Oceana, 1962). Unfortunately this detailed and sometimes bewildering guide to U. N. documentary sources is the only handbook of its kind.

Preceding the United Nations, the League of Nations had a similar literary output and bibliographic organization. The three most useful tools explaining its documentary materials are:

(a) Aufricht, *Guide to League of Nations Publications* (1951)

(b) Carroll, *Key to League of Nations Documents Placed on Public Sale 1920–1929* (with 4 supplements covering to 1936)

(c) Breycha-Vauthier, *Sources of Information: a Handbook on Publications of the League of Nations* (1939)

4. Documentation and Distribution Systems. International organizations often issue their documents in different forms for distribution. The forms of United Nations' publications are typical of this pattern. They include the following:

(a) *Mimeographed Document Series.* Most international organizations issue their documents initially in a provisional mimeographed form. It is in this series that they receive their identifying document numbers to which most publications cite. These documents comprise the most comprehensive and current set and a large proportion of them are not reproduced in any other form. Unfortunately, the mimeographed series are generally received only in the largest research libraries.

(b) *Official Records.* This series (much of which appears first in the mimeographed set) includes the corrected and final versions of documents which are designated as part of the official record of the particular organization or body. Records of debates and documents relevant to agenda items are included (reports of commissions, resolutions, etc.).

(c) *Sales Publications.* This series of documents includes those judged to be of wide public interest. They are available by subscription or individually and are given individual sales numbers for identification. They are usually printed, but occasionally appear in other processed form.

(d) *Depository Libraries.* These are designated to assure a wide distribution and use of the organization's documents. Such libraries contain all of the materials in (a), (b) and (c), except restricted and limited distribution material.

5.   International Court of Justice. Of particular interest in legal research are the publications of the International Court of Justice, which succeeded the Permanent Court of International Justice of the League of Nations. The I. C. J. meets at the Hague to settle legal controversies between countries and to resolve a limited number of other cases involving serious questions of international law. The publications of the I. C. J. include the following.

(a) *Reports of Judgments, advisory opinions and orders.* (Issued individually and in bound volumes in English and French texts).

(b) *Pleadings, oral arguments, documents* (same as above).

(c) *Yearbook of the I. C. J.:*

"Contains information on the composition of the Court (with biography of each Judge) . . . jurisdiction of the Court in contentious and advisory proceedings . . . it lists the states and others who are entitled

[*212*]

to appear before the Court and matters dealt with by the Court since 1946 together with summary of judgments and advisory opinions given during the course of the year . . . digests of the decisions relating to the application of the Statute and Rules, a bibliography of works published on the Court and relevant extracts from treaties, agreements and conventions governing the jurisdiction of the Court". Published in French and English editions.

6. Current Bibliographies. In addition to the foregoing documentary sources, references to recent publications in international law and relations can be found in the following bibliographic guides:

(a) *American Journal of International Law* (Quarterly). The bibliographic section of each issue is an invaluable source of information on current publications.

(b) *International Organization* (Quarterly). Each issue contains a useful bibliography on international organizations.

(c) *Foreign Affairs Bibliography* (Russell & Russell, 1933—). Comprehensive bibliographies published every 10 years.

(d) The Hague, Palace of Peace Library, *Catalogues* (Leyden, 1916—)

(e) Jacobstein & Pimsleur, *Law Books in Print* (Glanville, 1971 revision). Includes references to law books in English by author, title and subject. Updated by quarterly *Law Books Published.*

(f) Periodical indexes, such as *Index to Legal Periodicals, Index to Foreign Legal Periodicals* and *Harvard Annual Legal Bibliography.* (See Chapter IX above for details.)

7. Retrospective Bibliographies. The following reference books are useful sources for books on various aspects of international law:

(a) Robinson, Jacob. *International Law and Organization, General Sources of Information* (Sijthoff, 1967).

(b) Association of American Law Schools. *Law Books Recommended for Libraries* (Fred B. Rothman & Co., 1967–1970, 6 vols. looseleaf). Particularly "International Law." list no. 46.

(c) Harvard Law School Library. *Catalog of International Law and Relations* (1965–1967) 20 volumes.

FOREIGN LAW

Although foreign law has not been an important part of the practice of the average American lawyer and its sources rarely appear in most small law library collections, it is becoming an increasing concern of the legal profession. Increased foreign communication and trade have made the law of other countries important to life in this country and frequently relevant to legal proceedings in our courts. Business transactions between Americans and the citizens, companies, and government of foreign countries, have given rise to legal problems involving the laws of other countries. More and more American attorneys are required to prove the law of a foreign country in American court proceedings and many American legal scholars are now using foreign law as a basis for comparing and analyzing our own system.

The literatures of foreign legal systems parallel our own, but with significant differences. Most countries will have court reports, statutes, finding tools, periodicals and legal treatises, but their relative status and forms of publications may differ widely from ours. Bibliographic guides and general introductions are available in English for the law of some countries, but often foreign legal literature, outside of those countries which have adopted the English common law, remains an impenetrable mystery to most American legal researchers. Part of the bibliographic problem in dealing with foreign law stems of course from differences in language. Foreign legal dictionaries exist for many languages and they are collected in the major law libraries, but it is impossible to comprehend the law of an unfamiliar country in an unfamiliar language with only the aid of a legal dictionary.

1. Bibliographic Guides. A number of useful guides to foreign law materials have been published in English, among them the following:

(a) *Law Books Recommended for Libraries* (See above). This looseleaf compilation of bibliographies on different subjects has a number of sections devoted to the law of foreign countries. It is the single most comprehensive bibliography on foreign law, covering the most important sources in English and foreign languages.

(b) Szladits, Charles. *A Bibliography on Foreign and Comparative Law* (Oceana). This excellent tool includes books and articles in English. It consists of one basic volume published in 1955, supplemented by periodic cumulations, and is updated regularly in the *American Journal of Comparative Law.*

(c) Although there has not been a comprehensive guide to English legal materials (see section on English law below), the following handbooks, respectively on Australian and Canadian legal bibliography, are worthy of note:

> 1. Campbell, Enid. *Legal Research: Materials and Methods* (Sydney, Law Book Company 1967).
>
> 2. Christie, Innis, ed. *Legal Writing and Research Manual* (Toronto, Butterworth's, 1970).

(d) Szladits, Charles. *Guide to Foreign Legal Materials: French, German, Swiss* (Oceana, 1959). This bibliographic essay provides concise background information on these three legal systems and a highly selective critical bibliography. A number of similar guides by others have been published for different countries.

(e) UNESCO, *Register of Legal Documentation* (Paris, 2d ed., 1957). This is a country-by-country survey of the important legal sources throughout the world. Out of date, but still useful.

(f) *Law Books in Print* and *Law Books Published* (Oceana). See above. Includes many books on foreign law in English.

2. Periodical Guides. For periodical literature on foreign law, the following aids are helpful:

(a) Periodical indexes such as the *Index to Foreign Legal Periodicals, Index to Legal Periodicals* and *Harvard Annual Legal Bibliography*, all of which are discussed above in Chapter IX.

(b) Szladits, Charles. *A Bibliography on Foreign and Comparative Law*, described above, also indexes periodical articles.

(c) Blaustein, Albert. *Manual on Foreign Legal Periodicals and their Index* (Oceana, 1962) contains a list of important foreign legal periodicals with descriptive information.

3. Translations and Summaries of Foreign Law. There has been a growing literature on foreign law which includes many translations of actual laws, as well as discussions of law on different subjects for various foreign countries. For the simplest information, English summaries of the major areas of law of many countries appear annually in the fifth volume (*Law Digests*) of *Martindale and Hubbell's Directory*, arranged first by country and then by subject. Several commercially published series of foreign laws in translation are also available, prominent among which are *Digest of Commercial Laws of the World* (Oceana, five volumes, looseleaf); *American Series of Foreign Penal Codes* (Fred B. Rothman & Co., various dates); and a series of looseleaf volumes published by the Foreign Tax Law Association on the commercial laws and income tax laws of many countries. Similar publications have also been issued by official bodies, such as the Pan American Union (*A Statement of the Laws of* . . . *in Matters Affecting Business* covering various Latin American countries) and the U. S. Department of Labor (*Labor Law and Practice of* . . . countries throughout the world). In addition, several American accounting firms have been publishing series of brief guides to foreign tax and commercial law in English (e. g. Price, Waterhouse & Co., Arthur Andersen & Co., Ernst & Ernst, and Peat, Marwick & Mitchell). These are available from the issuing firm, sometimes on a complimentary basis. There is a useful compilation of the constitutions of the countries of the world: Peaslee, *Constitutions of Nations* (revised 3rd edition, 1965, four volumes). Another new such compilation is *Constitutions of the Countries of the World* (Oceana, looseleaf, 1971—).

ENGLISH LAW

Among all of the foreign legal systems, the one which is closest to our own is that of England. English law and tradition still have a special relevance in this country by virtue of our common Anglo-American legal development. The American colonies inherited the English common law and a legal tradition of statutes, cases, customs, and attitudes. Although since 1789 our own law has developed somewhat differently, we still share a heritage which often gives English law a persuasive value in our courts not generally afforded to the law of any other country. In addition, English legal scholarship, legislation and judicial decisions are frequently of considerable interest here.

The following is a brief outline of the main sources and forms of publication of English legal materials:

1. **English Statutes**

    (a) *Slip laws*, issued by Her Majesty's Stationery Office (H.M.S.O.)

   (b) *Session laws:*

      1. *Public General Acts and Measures* (H.M.S.O.). An annual chronological compilation of slip laws in 2 volumes with a non-cumulating subject index. This compilation also appears in the same form in the *Law Reports* series.

      2. *Current Law Statutes Annotated* (Sweet & Maxwell). An annual session law compilation, chronologically arranged, with annotations.

      3. *Butterworth's Annotated Legislation Series* (Butterworth). A *selective* annotated session law service.

   (c) *Halsbury's Statutes of England* (Butterworth, 3rd ed., 1968—). A well indexed subject arrangement of acts in force, supplemented with annual bound volumes and looseleaf service.

   (d) *Statutes Revised, 1235–1948* (acts in force arranged chronologically; latest edition unfortunately is still the 3rd, 1950).

   (e) *Statutes of the Realm*, 1225–1713.

(f) *Statutes at Large*, 1225–1869. Appears in various editions.

2. Statutory Indexes. The various session law compilations generally contain their own indexes and, in addition, the following compiled indexes are available for English statutes:

(a) *Chronological Table of Statutes* (H.M. S.O.). Covers 1235 to date; cumulated and revised annually.

(b) *Index to the Statutes in Force* (H.M. S.O.). This companion volume to the *Chronological Table of Statutes* above is cumulated and revised annually and provides an excellent subject index to English statutes.

(c) *Halsbury's Statutes of England* (Butterworth). Includes a consolidated index and individual volume indexes.

(d) *Statutes of the Realm* and *Statutes at Large* (alphabetical and chronological indexes).

3. Early Law Reports

(a) Earliest forms (*Plea Rolls, Yearbooks* and *Nominatives*). These are discussed in Chapter II above.

(b) *English Reports, Full Reprint* (W. Green, reprinted by Fred B. Rothman

& Co. and Stevens & Sons). Covers the major judicial decisions from 1378 to 1865 in 176 volumes, and includes an invaluable alphabetical table of cases in two volumes.

(c) *Revised Reports* (Sweet & Maxwell and Little, Brown & Co.). Covers 1785 to 1865 and partially overlaps the *Full Reprint*, but includes some cases not in it. Table of cases provided.

4. Current Law Reporting (1865 to date)

(a) *Law Reports* (Incorporated Council of Law Reporting for England and Wales, 1865 to date). These current series have semi-official status and authority; they include four reporters which cover:

> Appeal Cases
>
> Queen's Bench Division
>
> Chancery Division
>
> Probate, Divorce and Admiralty Division

(b) *Weekly Law Reports* (Incorporated Council of Law Reporting for England and Wales, 1953 to date). Most complete of all current English law reporting series.

(c) *All England Law Reports* (Butterworth, 1936 to date). Contains more decisions than the *Law Reports*, but not always with complete text.

(d) Special subject and topical reporters (similar to such specialized American reports).

5. Finding Tools

(a) *Current Law* and *Current Law Yearbook* (Sweet & Maxwell). This comprehensive research service includes a case digest and citator, statutory digest and citator, and a limited index to British legal periodicals and texts. It is issued in monthly pamphlets and annual bound volumes and is the most effective citator for English law. Separate editions are also published for Canada and Scotland.

(b) *English and Empire Digest* (Butterworth, Replacement Edition, 1961–1970). The most comprehensive and popular case digest.

(c) *Mews' Digest of English Case Law* (Sweet & Maxwell, 2nd ed., 1925–28, with supplements). The necessity of referring to two 10 year supplements (1925–35 and 1936–45) and individual annual supplements since 1945, makes this digest less useful than the *English and Empire Digest*.

(d) *Halsbury's Laws of England* (Butterworth, 3rd ed. 1952–1962). Despite its title, this is a general legal encyclopedia with references to case law, statutes, and administrative sources. It is well indexed, offers tables of cases and statutes cited, and provides cumulative annual supplements and a current looseleaf service.

(e) *Halsbury's Statutes of England* (Butterworth) See 1(c) above.

6. English Citators. There is no equivalent of Shepard's Citations for English legal bibliography, but the following tools, described above, offer various degrees of citator service.

(a) *Statutory citators*:

    1. *Current Law*

    2. *Halsbury's Statutes of England*

    3. *Mews' Digest*

(b) *Case citators*:

    1. *English and Empire Digest*

    2. *Current Law Citator*

    3. *Mews' Digest*

7. Bibliographies of English Law. As noted above, there are no comprehensive handbooks or treatises on English legal bibliography. The following bibliographies, however, are helpful for research in English law:

(a) Sweet & Maxwell, *A Legal Bibliography of the British Commonwealth of Nations*, (2d ed., 1955–1964, 7 vols.)

(b) *Guide to Law Reports and Statutes* (Sweet & Maxwell, 4th ed., 1963)

(c) *A Bibliographic Guide to the Law of the United Kingdom*, etc. (Institute of Advanced Legal Studies, 1956)

(d) Beale, Joseph H. *Bibliography of Early English Law Books.* (Harvard University Press, 1926; Supplement, 1943).

(e) Maxwell, Wm. Harold. *A Complete List of British & Colonial Law Reports & Legal Periodicals* . . . (Carswell, 3rd ed., 1937).

(f) *Where to Look for Your Law* (Sweet & Maxwell, revised periodically, last edition: 14th, 1962).

Despite their basic similarity of form, there are significant differences between the tools and methods of legal research in English sources and our own legal bibliography. Therefore, the fuller discussion in comprehensive treatises like Price & Bitner, *Ef-*

fective Legal Research and Pollack, *Fundamentals of Legal Research* is recommended here, as elsewhere, for more detailed information.

POSTSCRIPT

It is the author's hope that this *Nutshell* will be accepted for no more than what it is—the briefest of introductions to:

"The lawless science of our law,

That codeless myriad of precedent,

That wilderness of single instances."

INDEX

References are to Pages

INDEX

INDEX
References are to Pages

[235]

INDEX

INDEX
References are to Pages

[242]

[*245*]

INDEX
References are to Pages

INDEX
References are to Pages

[*251*]

STATUTES—Continued

United States Code Annotated, see *United States Code Annotated*

United States Code Congressional and Administrative News, see *United States Code Congressional and Administrative News*

United States Revised Statutes, see *United States Revised Statutes*

United States Statutes at Large, see *United States Statutes at Large*

Unofficial editions, 68–70, 77, 81, 91, 96

STATUTES AT LARGE (English), 222

STATUTES AT LARGE, UNITED STATES
See *United States Statutes at Large*

STATUTES OF THE REALM (English), 221–222

STATUTES REVISED, 1235–1948 (English), 221

SUBJECT REPORTERS, 33–34

SUPREME COURT BULLETIN, 21–22

SUPREME COURT DIGESTS, 35, 46, 102, 155, 183
See, also, Digests
Table of cases, 35
Table of statutes by popular name, 102
Table of statutes construed, 155
Treaty coverage, 183

SUPREME COURT REPORTER, 16–17, 23, 62
Advance sheets, 23
Exhibit, 16

SUPREME COURT REPORTS
See *Lawyers' Edition*
See *Supreme Court Reporter*
See *United States Reports*

TABLES OF CASES
American Digest System, 50–51
American Law Reports, 55

INDEX

References are to Pages

[*258*]

INDEX
References are to Pages